D0206460

WINE, MOON AND STARS

GÉRARD BERTRAND

WINE,
MOON AND STARS

Abrams, New York

Library of Congress Control Number : 2015931371

ISBN : 978-1-4197-1860-1

Original title : *Le Vin à la belle étoile*
Translation : Jane Anson

Visit us at www.editionsdelamartiniere.fr
Published in 2015 by Abrams, an imprint of ABRAMS

DESIGNER : NORD COMPO
PRINTING : NORMANDIE ROTO IMPRESSION S.A.S. (1604132)
LEGAL DEPOSIT : FEBRUARY 2015
Printed in France

115 West 18th Street
New York, NY 10011
www.abramsbooks.com

To Ingrid, Emma and Mathias
To Jean, Yann, Jean-Michel, Sophie and Virginie
To my family
To my colleagues
To my friends

Foreword

Gérard the Conqueror

Set high on a ridge above the Mediterranean Sea, overlooking the medieval village of Gruissan, is Château L'Hospitalet, where the air is heady with perfume dancing on the multitude of winds that blow in every direction. This is where Gérard Bertrand is known as *Le Grand*. The Tall Guy. With respect and more than a touch of admiration.

He stands at almost two metres tall and, *Le Grand* suits him perfectly, for obvious reasons. But in his case–and this is a man who is above all else a specific case–the word goes way beyond his physical appearance and sums up his whole personality. To me, Gérard Bertrand will always be Gérard the Conqueror, wielding a golden vine like a sceptre to rouse the Cathar spirits that still roam this region. William the Conqueror, King of England and master of a significant part of France, was born in Château de Falaise, set on one of the highest points in Normandy. And it's from another well-positioned château that Gérard of Occitan surveys his own empire of wine–from Narbonne in the Aude over to the heart of Catalan country in Tautavel, where *homo erectus* lived over 700,000 years ago and where the soil has nurtured the most profound complexities in the grenache grape for more than 15 centuries.

Gérard is an unusual mix of many men in one: a giant with arms strong enough to hold a family and a pack of friends, a heart big enough to offer comfort to those he meets along the way, the mental strength of a die-hard rugby player and, when required, a rock-star in the after-match bar or during his jazz festival at L'Hospitalet–a place that, by no coincidence, rhymes with hospitality.

Che Guevara's famous declaration to "be realistic, demand the impossible" could have been uttered by Gérard because in his own rather more peaceful way, he is every bit the revolutionary.

He is a master of the cosmos, at one with the stars as he walks through his vines at night. His words are by turn instructive–"The influence of the moon, sun and stars during a plant's growth cycle is fundamental, particularly those inner planets and celestial bodies closer to the Sun (the moon, Mercury, Venus and Mars) and to a lesser extent the outer planets (such as Jupiter and Saturn)"–or thought-provoking–"how many times have you heard parents telling their children not to eat stones? In reality, what children are doing subconsciously is the most natural thing in the world: tasting minerals to feel close to nature. I've never seen a child actually swallow a stone".

This is the place that Gérard most naturally inhabits, somewhere between realism and mysticism, certain in his belief that "nature knows best". Passing on the wisdom of a father to whom he owes so much, a man who was a referee on the rugby pitch at a time when the game could descend fairly regularly into little more than a free-for-all. Georges Bertrand allowed his son to discover the best rugby clubs of France as he followed him from match to match. Later, he grew into a valiant foot soldier for the game of rugby, revealing a huge talent for aerial combat and blessed with solid guts (in Marseille, they would speak of the essential accessories for any man).

Georges was also responsible for Gérard's first steps in the vines, setting him to work on his first vintage at age 10, with the words, "You know Gérard, you're lucky, because when you turn 50 you'll have had 40 years of harvests behind you". And now here he is, in the middle of his life, its "noon" as he so beautifully describes it, carried along by sincerity, by his love for the vine and by the people who, through drinking his wines, elegantly turn their throat into highways to happiness.

I have stayed with Gérard at his Cigalus estate many times over the past few years, surrounded by vines and the cicadas that inspired its name. His conversations with Ingrid, his remarkable wife–and remarkable you'd need to be to go toe-to-toe with a Gérard Bertrand–with their children Emma and Mathias listening in, made me appreciate the immense solidity of this man, this son of nature in full flow. The humour is quick-witted, barbed rather than comforting, because this is not a man to accept the slightest compromise. A full two metres in height and impossible to ignore!

There are many memories that I cherish: returning to the property with a hundred of his closest friends; a Field of the Cloth of Gold during the jazz festival at L'Hospitalet; under the kindly watch of the tiny Prunelle, the whirling dervish of a bulldog and the colossal Bounty, a bullmastiff who seemed as ancient and essential as Tautavel man. Here, sharing is everything, friendship all-enveloping; sharing a glass together is a religious gesture, offering respect to the blood of the earth.

To be counted among your friends, Gérard, is a source of great happiness, a draught of life. The bottle is always half full for me; replete with a wine where sunshine mixes with the moon. *Wine, Moon and Stars* sums you up perfectly. I toast our friendship, and I raise a glass to you!

Jean Cormier

Preface

Saint-André-de-Roquelongue, Narbonne, Corbières, the Minervois, the Languedoc, Roussillon, southern France.

The culture of our region has been created and shaped by these places, these lands, their histories and those of the men who have lived on them since the arrival first of the Romans, then the Visigoths and the Cathars. Its energy, spirit and soul has been an essential part of me since earliest childhood.

The Roman city of Narbonne, the Cathar city of Béziers, the Catalonian city of Perpignan, the fortified walls of Carcassonne, and more recently the contemporary vibrancy of Montpellier–all have forged their character over twenty centuries of rivalry, suffering and jealousies just as surely as through their irresistible welcome and southern *art de vivre*.

Winegrowers have found the South of France a fertile ground for economic, social and cultural development–as have rugby players. Bacchus was a constant presence throughout the lives of my grandmother Paule, my father Georges, my mother Geneviève, my uncle and my aunts. It would have been impossible for me to escape; it is part of our shared Occitan language, part of our DNA just as surely as the shores of the Mediterranean and the soils on which we stand.

Once a land of hunters and subsistence farmers, then of larger-scale producers before finally becoming a market economy, our winemaking region has a history of, as the saying goes, fighting yesterday's battles. Is it held back by an inferiority complex that it doesn't live up to the might of Bordeaux, Burgundy and Champagne? Or have we simply found that it is easier to play the part of the put-upon, swaggering upstart?

What a paradox to have created in 1531, at the Abbey of Saint-Hilaire in the Aude region, the world's first sparkling wine with the Blanquette de Limoux, and then 350 years later to have harnessed the energy of local producers in creating cooperative wine cellars and agricultural unions, and yet at the same time to have such difficulty explaining to the world, *urbi et orbi*, our history, our identity, our diversity, our truth–excepting one moment in 1907 during the winemakers' revolt led by Marcelin Albert. He became a popular hero at a time of crisis by demanding higher prices and a better future for our winemakers, but also indelibly branded our region with his image.

It was my father Georges Bertrand who taught me, from my very first harvest in 1975, the virtues of hard work, of paying attention to the thousand-and-one details that are essential to the production of quality wine. I've looked for excellence ever since. Each day I strive to improve on my skills and abilities, and each new vintage reinforces my convictions, my desires and my character. I want to prove equal to the best, worthy of my roots, my culture....This is far more than a career to me, but a declaration of faith; one that mixes *terroir*, technical skill, business aptitude, human resources, marketing, all in service of a shared vision and a determination to succeed.

The last 30 years have been a voyage of discovery. They have taught me the value of family life and given me an appreciation of meeting new people, of travelling, of tasting great wines, of the value of learning. We all want to make sense of our lives, and the dream is to achieve this while learning the value of love, respect, tolerance, a healthy sense of competition, and a desire to raise the bar.

Wine seems to achieve this feat both physically and spiritually, by affecting both our conscious and subconscious, spirit and soul, uniting thoughts and feelings, bringing people together, kick-starting conversations. And it is through the respectful hand of man that the vine, pruned back to life year after year by a series of careful gestures and choices, achieves a sense of harmony with its environment.

It took time to understand the subtleties of this work. Time to be in contact with the earth and the heavens, linked to my fellow winemakers through our communion with the vine; this plant that contains within it the aromas of countless fruits, revealing them to us through the simple transformation of its grapes into wine.

Twenty-five years ago, a meeting with homeopathic doctor Francis Mazel sparked the germ of an idea in me: to harvest my vines biodynamically. For the first eight years, we concentrated on Domaine de Cigalus, where a devoted, competent and passionate team practiced the teachings of Rudolf Steiner. After an initial baptism by fire, we saw the benefits to the vineyards, the diversity of nature that began to thrive within them, and the resulting quality in the glass.

We soon took the experiment to L'Hospitalet, La Sauvageonne and Les Karantes, then more recently to Tarailhan, Aigle, Aigues-Vives and La Soujeole, eventually introducing biodynamic farming across 350 hectares of our vines.

Biodynamics made me consider more deeply the question: "What is wine?". A hydro-alcoholic solution, a drink, a beverage, a cultural icon, a social lubricator, and a messenger, all rolled into one?

Understanding takes time and patience, and I have tried, after careful reflection, to set out the many facets of learning about wine, and how it links to our different physical senses. Each one offers the possibility of opening ourselves up to new experiences.

First there is pleasure: it is the basic emotion that we as winemakers need to guarantee our consumers. The sight, the smell, and the taste of the wine need to deliver the personality of the grapes that made it.

Beyond that, the taste should reveal the place of its birth and transcend the palate, that organ that Jean Cormier calls "the reservoir of happiness". Above all wine should emphasize its *terroir*, its regionality, its appellation of origin.

Stirring emotion is far more rare. Only the greatest wines travel directly to the heart, provoking that particular alchemy that comes from the perfect blend of friends and a wine served at the right temperature, in the right glass, and balanced by the perfect food.

And sometimes we are lucky enough to experience a truly ecstatic, transcendental experience where we meet a winemaker, visit and understand the *terroir* that has shaped him, and exchange views with him over old vintages of his wine.

I had the honour and privilege to experience this with Aubert de Villaine, owner and director of Domaine de la Romanée-Conti in Burgundy. This experience taught me to add a fourth dimension to my work–spirituality.

In 1997, while walking along the foothills of the Montagne Noire in the Herault, I came across a plot of *garrigue* by the commune of La Livinière bordered by low dry-stone walls, set just below the ruins of an old sheep farm. I had bought this magical spot just a few months earlier with Château Laville-Bertrou. It began my obsession with old-vine carignan and syrah, and was the perfect spot to add mourvèdre and grenache to create a wine with a true Mediterranean identity.

After 10 long years of reflection, exchanges, research and questioning, I decided to restore the old sheep farm and transform it into a winery, ensuring that it also contained a space for meditation and quiet reflection that its setting seemed to demand. This singular building, surrounded on all sides by vines and Mediterranean scrubland, has given this astonishing spot a sacred dimension that honours and builds on the potential of its *terroir*.

From this place was born Clos d'Ora.

The teachings of Rudolf Steiner, his understanding of the spectrum of life from the tiniest of details to the most infinite of concepts, his precise and detailed teachings in biodynamic farming, have been essential to me–as have certain complex, majestic wines, coaxed into being by the genius of their winemakers.

They have led me to question how the moon and the planets, and their interplay with the rocks and limestone in the soil, influence the taste of wine.

The essence of an exceptional wine is a combination of time, space, energy, spirit and soul. A great wine is connected to its *terroir*, to its grape variety, to the plot of land of its birth, but also to the universe that surrounds it. With this realization, I dared to experiment with a new path that links biodynamics with quantum theory.

While attempting to better understand the universe, I began to experience intuitions that seemed to be beamed directly to my soul, to the God particle that is in each of us. We all must find the strength to realize our potential–and the first step is wanting to do so. From the beginning, in the exceptional environment of Clos d'Ora, my intention has been to create a wine that delivers a message of peace, love and harmony. And here in the middle of my life, I felt the need to share with you my quest, and my love for this land of the Languedoc.

I

GETTING STARTED

1

My Roots

I was born in Corbières, a place with its own character and distinct identity, as well as a wine appellation in the Aude region of southern France.

"The Aude is France writ small", wrote historian and climatologist Emmanuel Leroy-Ladurie.

Certainly this region manages to cram an astonishing diversity of landscapes within its borders, from the shores of the Mediterranean to the foothills of the Pyrénées mountains. Water, sunshine, wind, mountains...everything seems exaggerated here, somehow nature is both magnified and returned to its essence. Only the vestiges of Roman, Visigoth and Cathar settlements remind us that this land has been tamed, forged and shaped both by and for us.

In winter, I love walking through the Vallée du Paradis up toward the *Citadelles de Vertiges*, so-named because the dizzying views from the battlements of these ancient fortresses literally make your head spin. First up are the ruins of Château Aguilar, dominating the horizon above Mont Tauch, where wild boars roam through the vines of Fitou. Next, passing through the tree-lined streets of Tuchan, I head toward the village of Cucugnan, a lost paradise where nature reigns. Here the year unfolds at its own leisurely pace, punctuated by harvests of local fruits and vegetables and hunting seasons for animals large and small. And in summertime, tourists spill out of cars and buses to visit Quéribus and Peyrepertuse, the two Cathar fortresses that border the village.

On windy days, the only way to make it up the endless stone steps that lead up to the main tower is by hanging on to the rope banister that climbs alongside you. I suggest visiting here alone, so you can absorb the stark beauty of this place that resisted the crusaders until 1255, the last bastion of Cathar resistance. Climb up to the summit, heart beating, breath ragged, and drink in the panoramic view of the Roussillon plain, then commune with the spirits that stalk these walls and dream of the destiny of the men who dared to take on the dogma of the Church, to be true to their own vision of Christianity.

Seven centuries later, the essential truth of their message can still take your breath away. Particularly if you are looking out over this landscape on a winter's day, pummeled by waves of wind, rain and freezing air, unable to resist the call to communion with the world before you.

It is impossible not to admire these men who braved the forbidden, took action against tyranny and spread ideas of freedom. They resisted the attacks of Simon de Montfort, the cruel nobleman who burned Cathars at the stake if they refused to give up their faith; or worse, as on one evening in Béziers when de Montfort and the abbot-commander Arnaud Amaury, unable to single out the pure from the impure, simply ordered his army: "Kill them all. God will recognise his own!"

In contrast, the peaceful behaviour of the Cathars saw them using reason instead of torture, preaching sermons, urging their followers to respect the word of God. They found a home and a fertile breeding ground for their doctrine at Château de Montségur in the Ariège region. This château stood firm against several attacks, and even today the ruins inspire the most profound respect. The Cathars also shared much of their teachings with followers in the city of Albi, which became the site of many fierce and terrifying battles where many lives were lost. Albi, along with Béziers, became pyres where countless of the faithful were burnt.

We are the descendants of these brave men. Our ancestors lived through these difficult years, first brought together by listening, learning, sharing, then torn through by violence, fear and terror. But while it is possible to temporarily quell the spirit, force people to renounce their beliefs and to submit to your will, the strength of the human spirit will always return, giving people the courage to fight, standing strong in the belief of God's love for each of us. We are connected to the universe and to nature through prayer but also through hard work, through the traditional act of cultivating the vineyards and olive trees that defines this Mediterranean land.

The Roman city of Narbonne was protected from the heresy of the Cathars. Its neighbour Béziers, in contrast, found itself at the very heart of the battle.

From 1960 to 1985, the symbol of this city was its rugby club, AS Béziers. The club's legendary trainer Raoul Barrière channeled the message of the Cathars to turn his much-garlanded rugby players into modern-day knights. They used a combination of power, technical skill and a shared desire to win to become conquering heroes, and as a result took home the Brennius Shield–given to winners of the French rugby union league, itself a symbol of a proud struggle–more than any other club over those three decades.

In 1974, 15 proud Narbonne men led by brothers Walter and Claude Spanghero and the genius of Jo Maso challenge their rivals Béziers in the final match of the championship and fail with Henri Cabrol's boot in the last few minutes of the game. The Languedoc supporters on both sides danced out of the Parc des Princes and through the streets of Paris in celebration of their region's prowess on the national stage. Alain Poher was serving as interim president at the time, a few months before stepping down after Valéry Giscard d'Estain's election to the office.

In 1979, Claude Spanghero, Lucien Pariès, François Sangalli and the rest of the team at RC Narbonne, after a calculated and precision-led attack, seized the trophy. I was a boarder at Collège Victor Hugo at the time, stuck all week behind thick stone walls breached by the sun only for four hours a day, between 11am and 3pm. On this particular Monday morning, we were surprised to see a troop of players and supporters outside our school courtyard, just off the train from Paris, drunk on joy and making merry. My dreams were awakened, and already I was imagining myself part of those all-conquering years alongside my brothers-in-arms from Narbonne.

From the age of five, as soon as I got home from school, I would throw my school bag to one side, grab a quick snack and run outside to replay Sunday's rugby match with my friends Serge, Régis and Angel. All our time was spent on the street, our rugby pitch marked by my uncle's house to the left and my parents' to the right. Our pitch was asphalt, with loose chippings that scraped our knobbly knees.

Six days out of seven, for at least two to three hours, we replayed those matches with passion, enthusiasm and boundless energy. That was where I practiced my scales; the art of the pass, the drop kick, learning how to outnumber the opposition in attacking or defensive play. We always wanted to be on the attacking side. As the youngest, I made up for my lack of height and weight by speed and dexterity–also known as avoidance measures.

Sunday was our only day off, when I followed instead the rhythm of my father Georges, a winemaker and broker during the week who reserved Sundays for indulging his own passion for the oval ball. He had enjoyed a successful career as a player at Carmaux, Perpignan and Bizanet, and now found that being a referee prolonged his joy at being out on the pitch, close to the game and its players. Rugby is not just a sport, it is an expression of a cultural identity. Béziers supporters were the powerful ones, Narbonne the rebels, Bayonne the bouncing Basques, Mont-de-Marsan the artists, Toulon the passionates, Nice the renegades, the Racing Club de France the white-collar workers, Brive the roughnecks, Montferrand the well-off...all squared up to each other every Sunday at 3pm kickoff.

Every other weekend, my mother, father and I headed off to one or other of these towns to follow the match. My sister Guylaine would stay behind to be cuddled by our wonderful grandmother. Through these trips I was lucky enough to get to know all the rugby stadiums around France before ever playing in them. I can remember being overwhelmed by the size of the players, drawn toward the powerful forwards but thrilled by the kinder players who stopped to give me an autograph. My father, who was known for his intransigence, loved the matches that turned into simmering battles, where the referee needed to keep the peace as much through the force of his personality as his whistle. Invariably these matches were expressions of virility, sometimes dangerously so. The different teams exchanged insults, and sometimes their darkest instincts got the better of them. Astre, Sutra, Fouroux, Pebeyre, later Gallion, Sanz Martinez, Élissalde; all were strong characters, goading their teams, inspiring the best of the forwards to send through a steady trickle of balls out to the wingers, keeping a strong hand against their opponents and the referee. The scrum halves played the role of general. They kept their troops in line with discipline, rigour and wisdom. Rugby is the school of life. After getting over the fear of seeing my father orchestrate this weekly Sunday afternoon battle, I was simply overcome by the fervour and the energy of the game.

How beautiful is the South of France as she celebrates this traditional exchange between sacred and sacrificed! Each Sunday, our ritual involved heading to mass at 10am, then to the bistro where we sat down to groaning plates of cassoulet, pigs' trotters, ham stew, and veal kidneys or beef casserole depending on the season and the local delicacies. Once we'd finished eating, it was time to head to the stadium to take our seats 30 minutes before the whistle. Enough time to check out the teams during the warm-up, and on derby days to trade insults with the team in the opposing stands.

Family meals depended heavily on sporting activities. My father was the youngest of nine children and my mother the eldest of eight, meaning we were lucky enough to grow up among a huge extended family, always part of a tribe celebrating together during marriages and communions. These family roots were an essential part of my development. Half of my family lived in Saint-André-de-Roquelongue, a small village with 813 inhabitants, the other half between Narbonne and Lézignan.

In summer, we liked to get on our bikes and head off to the swimming pool in Lézignan. Every day, with our group of friends, we would cycle 14 kilometres in one direction for a swim, then cycle 14 kilometres back in the other. In the village, as soon as the weather permitted it, we spent all our time outside. There was no television, and anyway the girls liked to play hopscotch, and the boys *pétanque*.

In winter, before our evening meal, we would congregate at my grandmother's house for a family get-together. We only spoke Occitan. Politics was forbidden in an attempt to avoid arguments between my various uncles and aunts, with the radical socialists on one side and the *gaullistes* nationalists on the other. Passions ran high, particularly after a few homemade quinquinas. Better to stick to rugby or winemaking, where everyone was in agreement.

After coming home from the Algerian War, my father became a wine broker and made plans for growing the local cooperative cellar in the village. He decided to run for its presidency but was beaten, no doubt because his ideas were too experimental. This defeat turned out to be the making of him; he negotiated instead the purchase of

Domaine de Villemajou from the Caillard family and in 1973 began making his first ever vintage.

Having spotted the potential of this *terroir* near the town of Boutenac, where torturously old Carignan vines turned out a divine nectar, Georges Bertrand became one of the first to use whole-bunch fermentation for the carignan grapes on the advice of Jean-Henri Dubernet. This technique emphasised the taste, aroma and power of the variety.

Large red stones line the vineyards in this part of Corbières. A few second-hand barrels bought from prestigious Bordeaux châteaux allowed him to experiment with aging wines in oak. It took courage to work toward achieving true quality in a region where most grapes were sold in bulk to wine merchants, destined to become table wine for easy drinking, sometimes even blended with wines from Algeria or Italy. My father believed that there were local grape varieties whose worth was underestimated and that were capable of revealing a sense of place, had a taste that was worth seeking out, and that displayed a growing confidence in the appellation.

As the local wine trade did not exactly welcome this new development with open arms, my father and a few friends–including Yves Barsalou, future president of Crédit Agricole bank–decided to create a new style of wine cooperative that they called the Société d'Intérêt Coopératif Agricole.

It was the beginning of a thrilling adventure for the region–and one that gave it a new sense of dynamism. They kept things simple at first: offices were on the ground floor of our family house, a kind of financial laboratory with my mother as secretary. There were just two extra pairs of hands. Each morning, they would taste several hundred wines, write detailed notes on them and rank them. In the afternoon, they would head out to Narbonne, Béziers, Beaucaire or Sallèles-d'Aude to start making sales. Throwing off the shackles of the wine merchants was basically impossible. What they needed to do instead was to convince them, slowly but surely, that these wines were different, elegant, refined, with an honest sense of place. Midi wines had a pretty catastrophic image at the time, little better than dishwater, so they had their work cut out for them.

Being at least 20 years ahead of the curve caused plenty of problems for Georges, who sometimes cultivated misunderstandings, jealousies and ill-feeling. Many did not understand why he would want to change a system that might have had little future but was comforting and reassuring to the majority of winemakers who lived as hunter-gatherers, according to the seasons of the vine, hunting, fishing, pétanque and the annual August holiday on the beaches of Port-la-Nouvelle, otherwise known as "Corbières beach".

Getting started is always tough. You need to have total belief and be willing to knuckle down for a better future. My father began to produce wine using modern techniques, defining specific styles for each different *terroir*. He took his message out first to local restaurants, then quickly went further to national supermarket buyers. The first stirrings of success arrived. The wine of Domaine de Fontsainte, owned by family friend Yves Laboucarié, was served to the French president at the Elysée Palace. I can still remember the reaction when the local paper published the news. Things were changing.

2

Apprenticeship

I needed to get involved. I was 10, my sister Guylaine 15 months older. Our mother took charge of the harvesting team while our grandmother, at 75, was still out there in the vines, secateurs in hand. Clearly we wanted to help out. First over the weekends, then for a couple of weeks at a time. It was my father who made the decision: Guylaine in the vines and Gérard in the cellar. I helped, in a very small way of course, to vinify my first vintage in 1975. The fact that I was so small at the time turned out to be pretty useful for climbing into the tanks to clean them, sort through the grape skins once the juice had been squeezed out, empty them out and ensure everything was put back in the right place. I spent up to 10 hours a day with the team, watching everything, particularly the astonishing rigour and attention to detail of my uncle Paul Griffoul, who worked as cellar master. My father would stop by, taste the wines and hand out instructions. I tried to understand the alchemy in front of me: how tasteless grapes could transform in just a few days into intensely coloured wine, rich in aromas both powerful and delicate. It seemed like nothing so much as a magic trick.

Every night when I got back home, the air would be scented with the exotic aromas of Spanish food that had overtaken the village. Groaning plates of fried potatoes and Iberian ham were being prepared for supper by the 500 Spanish harvesters who had settled in for three weeks. I inhaled my own dinner and headed out to meet my friends to replay the Spanish-French football match. The rivalry was fierce. The Spanish may have been technically more proficient, but we had the home-side advantage. Matches often lasted two hours and involved several generations of players. We never tried to play rugby against them, as most had never even seen an oval ball before!

After 15 happy days in the cellars, it was time to get back to school. On my last day, my father came to find me. I climbed up into his car and he turned to look at me, saying, “You know Gérard, you’re lucky, because when you turn 50, you’ll have had 40 years of harvests behind you”. He was right–we only get one chance each year to do the harvest, so we may as well start as early as possible. His words took on even greater significance in October 1987, when we lost him to a car crash. I was 22 at the time. My military service with the Joinville Battalion–rugby corps–was over. I had officially started working in the family company three months earlier but wanted to have enough free time to be able to also pursue my passion for rugby, which had turned into a spot for the previous two years with the Narbonne Racing Club, my home team and one of the elite of the French game.

Destiny had something else in store. On November 2, with the blessing of my mother and sister, I opened the doors to our five employees and announced that I would be taking over. There was no time for doubts–I had to be ready.

On the evening of October 27, after dinner, my father had said to me, “Get some rest, then we need to talk”. He talked about his vision for winemaking and offered advice on my burgeoning career, in rugby as well as wine. I headed off to bed a couple of hours later than usual, buoyed by his confidence. My father had a strong personality, and it was always easier for me to listen to him than to discuss things as equals. Yet somehow he had sensed that he needed to pass on his final words of wisdom.

Five years earlier, in 1982, he had been profoundly affected by a break with the winemakers of Septimanie, the company that he had been heading up. Slowly but surely he had begun to imagine a different future than the one pursued by a company that had seen impressive growth but had begun to set aside the idea of wines of origin in favour of the siren call of the markets.

Georges Bertrand's vision–a pyramid built on the expression of *terroir* and of added value–was shared by a minority, but it became increasingly difficult to put into practice. He had a few early successes, but it is tough to be a forerunner and hold true to your beliefs when those around you are not responding as you would like. It's still more difficult if you are trying to safeguard the interests of all. In the end he left to return to the family property, while flexing his commercial instincts by joining one of the best brokerage companies in the region. Happily, close family and rugby friends helped to refocus his priorities and also laid the groundwork for my arrival on the team. He began to work as a consultant for a few merchants who were looking to increase quality, and his experience and skill were in growing demand.

That last night, October 27, he told me he believed the best model for future growth lay with the family companies where shared vision could build lasting success. He drew on successful examples of great French winemaking families such as Moueix, Guigal or Dubœuf, and Torres, Mondavi or Antinori internationally.

I learnt a lot more over the course of the many dinners my mother organised with our importers, and at the same time tried to drink in the poetry and the memory of my father through his wines. It was at this point that I met Alain Favereau, one of the best tasters in France. He has spent 45 years with the Nicolas chain of wine merchants and it was to be 15 years until I saw him again - still tasting with the same professionalism, rigour and attention to detail, and still displaying the same encyclopedic knowledge of wine.

Wine taster or wine lover? The latter believes that wine should be drunk with food, and will always evaluate its worth over the course of a meal.

When I was growing up a family lunch would invariably involve assessing one of the many blends prepared by my father. My mother and sister's opinions were often sought, as women generally are more sensitive to bitterness and give more spontaneous feedback. One comment about a bitter taste was enough to send him back to the drawing board, and I continue the tradition today by asking the opinion of my wife Ingrid and children, Emma and Mathias.

A wine either is, or is not, in balance. Deciding which it is takes us into the subtle realm of feelings mixed with rigorous attention to detail. I used to love tasting and blending sessions with my father. The best school is at the feet of an expert, and this was an apprenticeship in a time that was tougher than today, where advances in oenology were significant and continual, and where each advance opened the door to unknown territory. The key names were Émile Peynaud, Jean-Claude Berrouet and Michel Bettane. Lalou Bize-Leroy was the conscience of wine, the guardian of the temple of Romanée-Conti; Nicolas Joly, the gateway to biodynamic farming, and Jancis Robinson the female voice of wine.

At the time, Robert Parker was still in law school and English critics such as Hugh Johnson and Steven Spurrier ruled the world. The conquest of the world, its globalisation, was just taking its first steps. In California, one man was embodying this new El Dorado: Robert Mondavi. He introduced a new way of speaking about wine through its grape variety–more straightforward and less mysterious than talking about *terroir*. The competition heated up, and it seemed all the powerful countries in the world were suddenly developing a taste for red wine and turning it into gold. Japan developed a deep respect for French wines. The Chinese woke up to the prestige of Bordeaux. The global image of France helped enhance the reputation of Bordeaux and Champagne, which in turn meant easier access to international markets for the wines of Sancerre, Beaujolais and Côtes du Rhône.

The Midi was still largely marginalised as a producer of table wines, but there were stirrings of a happier future. A couple of enlightened dreamers, whether by intuition or experience, began to unlock the potential and the first pages of a new chapter were written. But there remained the rest of the book to complete.

The South of France wine category was far from organised. On the one side were those who championed the grape variety. Its most vocal champion was Robert Skalli, the first to really understand the vast potential of the Languedoc to produce wines that could meet international expectations. In the other corner were the traditionalists, who believed that there would be no success without *terroir*. Standing up for tradition–alongside my father and his band of Corbières winemakers - were the JeanJean brothers, Jacques Berges-Grulet, Aimé Guibert and André Cazes. For them, chateau bottling was an essential guarantee of origin and a reassurance to our consumers.

As these events were unfolding, two challenges had me particularly fired up: becoming champion of France in rugby, and showing the world just how good the wines of our region could be. I decided to try my hand at both.

One morning in the winter of 1993, as I was just setting out to do a quick tour of the vineyards, I received a phone call. "Hi Mr. Bertrand. I am Christophe Blanck, new buying director of the Carrefour Group. I have been hearing good things about you and would love to meet up". He came down south to meet me and we spent a full day together, visiting wine cellars and tasting over 100 samples. I explained that I was both a winemaker and consultant for a few prestigious estates. He then asked me if I would like to be the talent spotter of Languedoc-Roussillon wines for Carrefour. "We have to rework our range and offer better quality wines. What I'd like you to do is to taste the wines produced by local merchants and let us know what you think of them". I accepted the offer, knowing immediately that it might cause a few ripples in the region. I selected quality wines and was unsparing in my opinion of the rest. I received a few threats but I've got broad shoulders and could take the heat, knowing that what I was doing was for the greater good, advancing the renown of the whole region on the shelves of the second biggest distributor in the world. I took the role seriously, but after two years stepped back with the intention of developing my own range.

3

Rugby: The School of Life

For eight years I lived a double life; sportsman on one hand, wine professional on the other. My first steps toward being a rugby player had started in my village streets, then continued in the rugby school run by my uncle Paul Bertrand. Joining together with my father, he had taken over a local club that had been left to gather dust in the years after the war. Georges took care of the sporting side and Paul the rest.

This part of my life was lived through the passion of these two very different brothers. My father was a people person. He was able to motivate the players, fire them up for combat. It was tough at first. The ground was dry, the soil was in bad condition, the pitch was overrun with a stubborn weed known as quackgrass. Summer saw the profusion of *goussets*–hard clumps of vegetation–that could slice right through your muscles if you fell on them.

Rugby training took place in the evenings. From October onward, the pitch was lit by the light of the moon. My father introduced training sessions where we did not once touch a ball. The players, many of them just getting started in the sport in a serious way, became serious athletes through his cross-training sessions. One evening the training grounds were flooded, but instead of sending us home we set out on a cross-country run through vineyards, dirt tracks and roads, running in our rugby boots, crampons pounding.

Feet bloody, we eventually returned to the changing rooms. I was 12 and did everything right alongside the older players, something that was hugely important for my personal development. I liked being with adults, the idleness of adolescence seemed a waste of time. I wanted to grow up, make my own choices, join in this great adventure. My heroes were Henri, Claude, Patrick, Antoine, Alain, Jean-Paul and the rest of the team who were in turn led by Georges.

Rugby is full of life lessons, from the importance of teamwork to learning how to live successfully alongside different characters. Everyone needs to head in the same direction, share in the delirium of success and the pain of failure. The holy grail in this case was becoming champion of France in our category. Twice, my village team lost in the final. We made it the third time around, after two matches and an even scoreline at the final whistle of 12-12. It had been impossible to choose between Saint-André, the men of Corbières, and those of Coursan, the town that produced much of the local wines. But we couldn't let it lie; the Brennus Shield waited for whoever did the best job of convincing the officials that the win should have been theirs. My father headed up to the podium with the captain to fiercely argue his corner with the match delegate, whom I heard say, "If you want the Shield so much, take it". He did not need telling twice, and handed it over to the captain who placed it triumphantly, on June 12, 1982, on the pitch of Stadium Albert-Domec in Carcassonne. The crowd went wild, and the partying continued for the rest of the summer.

At 11, I started boarding school in Narbonne and joined the rugby club, where I quickly made captain. Seeming older than my years must have helped, and I enjoyed leading the team to a few successes but also numerous failures. We were a good team without any particular magic formula. That was not the point. Our training had begun. We played against the best teams in the region while trying to outdo our rivals Béziers, doing our best to learn from the techniques of the teams that stood above us. We needed to learn how to pass and tackle but also how to challenge our opponents. Mastering each individual element is essential for maintaining the edge in a match. Getting physical was allowed, even going so far as intimidating your opponent, maybe even launching the odd swipe on their nose. The spectators on the sidelines would shout at us to "get stuck in". After the match it was time for a communal shower. We would dress our wounds then meet up for a drink in the clubhouse. When the best players were competing on a regional level, local rivalries would disappear in the hunt for a national trophy.

We shared the sweaty locker room, the pre-match incantations, then bonded further over 80 minutes on the battlefield. We were driven by shared passion and a sense of adventure, and a desire to conquer the world. By the age of 19 I had made it to the juniors. A few weeks earlier, my first pair of contact lenses had cleaned up my eyesight, and a match against Béziers made me realise my potential. André Delpoux, the grandfather of my future winger buddy Marc, called my father and said, "Gérard will soon be playing in the first team. I saw him on Sunday and he's going to be ready soon". Six months later I was on the team.

After finishing my studies at agricultural college in Carcassonne, I joined the first year of a business administration and sport studies course in Toulouse. This is where I met Mr. Bru, otherwise known as Robert the Scientist, who conceived and developed, with the help of Pierre Villepreux and Jean-Claude Skrela, the fundamentals of Toulouse rugby. He helped shape my technical game and opened my eyes to the power of movement, something that came to be known as "French flair", the art of assuring continual movement and improvisation across the pitch. I quickly got the idea and was selected for the French university team where I was lucky enough to play alongside legendary sportsmen like Franck Mesnel and Denis Charvet, already stars in France and on pitches across the world.

We had a fantastic tournament in the United Kingdom led by coach Olivier Saisset with his relentless, straight-talking and hugely effective management style.

At the end of the season, I joined Narbonne and began to earn my spurs on the team. You had to elbow your way in, because competition was fierce, particularly during training sessions. I was carried along by a hunger for success and by the mule-headedness forged in a childhood spent among the hills of Corbières.

What a talented generation of players. Our president, Bernard Pech de La Clause, teamed up with Jean-Louis Despoux in an attempt to entice the "wizard" Raoul Barrière to be our trainer. He had long been a legend to our neighbours in Béziers, and the results when he joined us were as rapid as the methods were unusual. The rhythm of our training sessions and warm-ups all changed. We spent three hours twice a week at the stadium, effectively doubling what we had done before. The moments before heading out onto the pitch for a match were spent practicing a dynamic relaxation technique known as sophrology. The team spirit was cemented. Natural leaders abounded, with different sections of the team headed up by two exceptionally talented men; Francis Dejean for the forwards and Henri Sanz for the wingers. Sanz was also captain, because he played scrum-half and directed the operation from inside. Coming from Graulhet in the Tarn, he was already an outsider to the region and was sturdy, sharp-eyed, a warrior–a leader in unshakeable physical condition with a strong-jawed determination that was impossible to ignore. Dejean came from the town of Foix the Ariège region. He came to the club through a recommendation of a friend there, and we knew very little about him at first. He put on the number 4 jersey for the first time in our first match against Mont-de-Marsan. For the next 14 seasons, no one took it off him.

After 10 minutes playing'time and the third scrum, he asked our hooker Robert Nivelle, "What's the code here?" The reply was,

"There's no need for a code on this team". Ten seconds later, the opposing team's hooker was laid out flat on the floor and Dejean's career was underway. He played rugby as if he was squaring up for battle, projecting such an aura of confidence and brute force that he shone, bringing huge confidence to the rest of the team. He was utterly fearless. Standing beside Gilles Bourguignon, the two of them made an impenetrable and complementary lock.

Soon we were thirsty for victories and recognition; we wanted to be remembered. We got as far as the semifinal against Agen in 1988 and against Toulon in 1989; losing the first, unjustly, because of a few blows of the referee's whistle, then more fairly against Toulon the following year. We won the Yves-du-Manoir Challenge three years in a row against Biarritz, Grenoble and Bègles–a competition that, as far as players are concerned, is equal to the French Cup at this level. The European Cup did not exist yet, and these titles carried with them a strong symbolic value. We had a reputation for playing tough, preferring to attack rather than defend. We enjoyed both provocation and a good challenge. "Better to be feared than loved" was our motto. Refereeing was less tight than it is today, and you had to earn respect in every rugby ground across the country. Murray Mexted, of the famous All Blacks, had arrived a few years earlier to play for Agen, and said, "In France, if you end up in the opposition half, you'd better be prepared to die for your homeland".

Teeth knocked out, knees in the chest; it was all part of a daily routine not exactly encouraged but tolerated; turning a blind eye was all too common. During one of my first matches against Béziers, I committed the sacrilege of falling over in the opposition's half. Retribution was swift: Diego "the Minataur" Minaro smashed two of my ribs. Five minutes later, after catching my breath and gathering my thoughts, I got back on the pitch and finished the half.

The rules of the game are not exactly the same as the ones you'll find written in the official Rugby Union rule book–and anyway I have yet to meet a player who has opened the first page. I was the exception and learnt them by heart. As the son of a referee, I quickly saw the benefit of understanding what was and was not allowed; it could give me a few seconds' advantage over my opponent, a precious ability to anticipate events and their potential outcome. Rugby, invented by the English, is, in the words of Jean-Pierre Rives, "a hooligan's game played by gentlemen". Mutual respect is always restored after the final whistle, but for 80 minutes on the pitch it is outright war.

In the 1990s, the sport was still governed by the rules of amateur rugby. We were very happy, twice a week, to get together to prepare for Sunday's match. Saturday I would rest up so as to be full of energy for the next day. The weeks passed quickly, marked out by the seasons, particularly during harvest time. I was living alone, a little reclusive, allowing myself the occasional night out after a big victory.

Between the ages of 22 and 29, I juggled being both CEO of my own business and a professional sportsman. I had the great fortune to be chosen to represent France, playing with the French Barbarians. I got to travel widely, meet new people, expand my horizons and have a great time. I was humbled to have earned the respect of my teammates and opponents. The final scoreline was less important than the human adventure born of combat, shared experiences, victories, failures and almighty celebrations. We learnt how to push ourselves in all respects and to live on the edge with the express aim of understanding ourselves better. In turn, this attitude improved team spirit and also reinforced our self-confidence.

I never lifted the Brennus Shield. At the end of my professional career, I accepted that it would be one dream that would not be realised. My career in Narbonne afforded me the huge privilege of playing for two seasons alongside Didier Codorniou, the Maradona of rugby–almost certainly the first player to instinctively play quantum rugby. Jonny Wilkinson was another, although his approach was perhaps less intuitive and more studied. Codorniou had the ability to change direction in a fraction of a second, to find the gaps, create a breach in places where opponents would fear to go. He gave a new meaning to space and time. His precision, needle-like ability to pass and unending ability to change course defied the laws of gravity. He was Mozart in a rugby shirt. He was born for this game and thrived in its presence.

I also crossed swords with several giants. Philippe Dintrans, the world's best forward for several years, a guts-and-glory player and true warrior who gave his all and was rewarded as top dog; Éric Champ, the rebel, the soul of Toulon, the gladiator, unblinking in the face of any challenge. And many others...The list of those I enjoyed sparring with is long.

I sometimes can hardly believe that it was anything other than a dream. Today the page has turned, the book is closed. I regard this whole period as a toast to the enthusiasm of youth, the power of the group, the bonds of friendship, and to lessons learnt along the way. A new chapter in my life was waiting once I decided to end my career at the Stade Français in Paris.

4

Reconversion

My time at Narbonne was fleeting. It was not an easy decision to make but it was time to make way for the next generation, that of Labit, Belzons and others who now held the future of the club in their hands. After 17 years, I announced my intention to leave to my captain, Henri Sanz, the night of our quarterfinal defeat against Castres. My business was growing, and my body was starting to show serious signs of fatigue. I opened an office in Paris and offered my services to the Stade Français to help them move back toward the elite of the country's game. Alongside my friend Jean-Baptiste Lafond, one of the most talented players of our generation, we moved back up to the first division. Mission accomplished, after two sinus operations and a red light delivered by the doctors as to the future of my career. I had come full circle.

As this final part of the adventure developed, I met Max Guazzini, a great president; intelligent, visionary and gifted with an innate sense of marketing and brilliant communication skills. He not only succeeded in bringing his team back up to the highest level, but through his singular vision, he also pushed the entire sport in a new direction. He broke the rules, changed received ideas, ignored taboos, cultivated aesthetics, beauty, the virility of attack, and also created a solid team that was ahead of its time. These were the keys to the club's success, and they then spread across French rugby, allowing it to become a true spectator sport. Women and children were finally welcome in the stadium, with the action starting an hour before kick-off and finishing an hour after the final whistle. Welcome to Max's world. His genius lay in knowing how to harness the values of rugby, not only for the initiated but also for simple lovers of the sport. I was injured and on the bench for six months during my last season, and took the time to study his performance. He did nothing without careful behind-the-scenes planning, meticulous mental preparation.

Over dinner one night, Max shared his idea of making a recording of classic rugby songs from after-match celebrations, including a couple of his own private creations. He told us that he wanted us to sing them, so after two months' rehearsal, our group Les Dropers were out doing the rounds of television and radio stations with our *Ce Soir On Vous Met Le Feu (Allez Le Stade)*, which sold enough to go gold, and is still sung in stadiums and nightclubs in France. A great combination of teamwork, professionalism and fun.

My year in Paris also allowed me to get to know several key supermarket buyers. One of these, Jean-Pierre Andlauer from the Monoprix group, tasted my wines and explained that Corbières was to be tasted by the team from the restaurant guide Gault Millau. It was not easy waiting for the feedback, but eventually we heard good news: the wine was selected for their permanent range. Henri Gault, one of the most eminent food critics in France, had founded the celebrated magazine with his colleague Christian Millau. In spring of 1995 he travelled down to visit me with Andlauer. I carefully prepared a dozen wines to taste. The meeting took place at 10am in the cellars of Domaine de Villemajou. The tasting began, with the wines lined up like models along a catwalk. After an hour and a half of note-taking, the verdict was given. "I've selected 11 wines," said Henri Gault. I tried not to be too effusive with my response; me, a tiny winemaker who had only just enlarged his range of southern wines. The buyer tried to say that was too high a number but Gault stuck to his guns. "These wines are the future. They are fresh, accessible, and taste of the terroir. We need them". For several years, Monoprix was not only my biggest client globally but helped me hone my skills as a winemaker.

Johannesburg, June 24, 1995, 3am. I was with my friends Pierre and Jean-Pierre, celebrating with a few whisky-and-Cokes in a buzzing nightclub. A few hours earlier we had been part of an historic afternoon; the South African team had beaten New Zealand in the final of the World Cup and the "rainbow nation" was being healed before our eyes. Whites and blacks were dancing together in the streets, singing together and celebrating this day of grace made possible by Madiba, Nelson Mandela. After his long years of suffering and isolation, he had forgiven his oppressors, silenced the hate and ushered in a new era for this divided nation. The film *Invictus*–even if a little caricatured in parts for rugby fans–perfectly captures the complicity shared that day by the Springboks and the South African nation.

The values of rugby are best expressed in sharing, solidarity, brotherhood and a good dose of humility. The scrum is a symbol of the power of the group. A mass of flesh and bone, soldered together in pursuit of the ball, allowing the whole team to push forward into the opposition half. This effort, this brotherhood and collective force is often invisible to onlookers but is a hymn to team spirit, to the power of collective effort, to the importance of self-sacrifice for the common good. The group takes precedence over the individual at all times in rugby. Fear gives way to courage and each step forward creates heroes who, inch by inch, find the space to drive toward to the line of attack.

The atmosphere in the stadium that day was unparalleled. President Nelson Mandela saluted both teams while dressed in the South

African team shirt. The All Blacks were dumbfounded, in awe of his charisma. The crowd was delirious. History would call this a defining moment for the nation. Even the New Zealand team, perhaps not playing at its best, had the good grace to simply enjoy the historic nature of the victory.

I shared the emotions of the evening with François Sangalli, an ex-Narbonne player, and we began discussing my vision for the future of our former club. At 4am, Narbonne's new president Jean-Louis Barsalou joined in the conversation in this far-flung corner of the world. François shared my views for the club's future and there was no going back. Destiny was set.

So, one month later, at 31, I found myself part of the management of Narbonne, and its president one year later. It took three years to get it to a position to rival the best, and along the way I picked up yet more powerful life lessons that set me in good stead for my future. I quickly learnt, notably, that you cannot run the finances of an association that has shared ownership the same way you can those of your own company. There is a political dimension, a need for diplomacy that as a young man I was rarely able to understand. Presidents are only passing through, and their mandate needs to be worthwhile. After three years of hard work, I gave way to my successors, having, I hope, successfully steered the club into the professional era. My future lay elsewhere.

5

Transition

My year in Paris strengthened my conviction that my future lay in the South of France. I found it tough to imagine living in a big city long-term, despite the numerous charms of Paris, the most beautiful city in the world. I was called home by my farming roots, by the need to centre myself, by my taste for silence. Paris was a necessary step on my journey, but from now on short but regular visits would be enough to satisfy both my needs and those of my business. Inevitably, my rugby contacts were enormously helpful in filling out my address book. This process was known as social advancement and was usual in the world of amateur rugby.

One night, a little worse for wear following a couple of post-match drinks, my friends Claude Spanghero, Dominique Erbani, Daniel Dubroca, Jean-Patrick Lescarboura, Philippe Saint-André, Jean-Baptiste Lafond, Jean-Luc Joinel, Philippe Sella, Laurent Cabannes, the brothers Camberabero, Stéphane Graou, Pierre Rougon, José Mateo, Jacques Fouroux and I decided to start a club of former rugby players who had gone on to work in the food and wine business. Our idea was to sell turnkey promotional schemes to distribution chains. We would offer products of *terroir* such as foie gras from the Gers, cassoulet from Castelnaudary, raviolo from the village of Romans in the Rhone-Alps, Pyrénées cheese, local seasonal fruits, as well as a large range of wines from the South of France, together with Champagne and coffee–in other words, an abundance of culinary and viticultural *savoir faire*. Casino supermarket decided to take a chance on us and set up meetings with both clients and staff. We were invited to Besançon in the Franche-Comté for a "high mass". Patrick Sébastien, the most in-demand TV host in France, joined us and immediately showed that he not only shared our love of rugby but also our enjoyment of good food and wine. We played a match against the local team and mingled with the large crowd who had come to watch. That night, invited to the town's meeting hall , we put on a show in front of 6,000 people who had come to welcome us and enjoy the mastery of Sébastien. Again we learnt of the power of shared communication, of what a club can achieve if all of its members work together. We did good business that night, each of us strengthened by the success of our neighbour.

The next morning on the train home, we named our group the "Rugby Gastronomes". For the next four years we globe-trotted–or, more accurately, went on the Tour de France–around all the major players. Carrefour, Leclerc, Système U, Auchan and Intermarché all bought into both our concept and identity. It was hugely fun, with legendary evenings hosted by Jacques Fouroux where we talked about everything and everyone. I have never met anyone as charismatic and enveloping as Jacques, the prince of Gascony. He always had something to fight for, a cause to defend, together with an unrivaled ability to move hearts and minds. My business boomed through this food fest and at the same time I was making contacts at the very highest level of the French distribution network. In the showers after an exhibition match that we played near Lyon against our distributors, I heard one buyer say, "Well, that's the first time that I have seen the bare arse of a supplier". A great sign of closeness...

As far as my wine business was concerned, the essential questions were focused around strategy, objectives and means. Identifying my priorities would take a little time. I decided to learn through trial and error; not always getting it right, but learning lessons. The only things I knew for sure were that I would never compromise the quality of my wines, and that I would always think globally, not just in terms of France or Europe. That meant traveling, observing, trying to understand the rules of the so-called "emerging markets". I also began physically buying more properties. Having neither great personal wealth nor an abundance of investors in my company, I quickly learnt how to develop good relations with the banks.

Growth was pretty quick, with successive purchases of, in 1995, Domaine de Cigalus; in 1997, Château Laville-Bertrou and in 2002, Château L'Hospitalet. This last purchase was made possible through the precious support of Patrick Colomb, who became my financial advisor. Our first meeting took place on the sidelines of a rugby pitch. He must have taken pity on me. He more typically advised international companies such as Essilor, or the big Burgundy estates, but for some reason decided to help me. I remember him looking sideways at me with the words, "Well, Gérard, there is work to be done". He got my affairs in shape both legally and financially, to ensure that banks would take me seriously and allow the company to expand to the next level.

When Jacques Ribourel, owner of L'Hospitalet, called me at the end of 2001 and suggested meeting up, I had no idea that he was going to ask if I wanted to take over his château; mainly because I did not have the necessary money. But he had lost a lot over the previous 10 years through launching his avant-garde concept of wine tourism. His ideas were proved right, of course, but he was too far ahead of the curve, and efforts to continue doing it justice were suffocating him. Patrick's help was essential for keeping negotiations on track while also convincing the right financial institutions to back me in the adventure.

My head was spinning from the idea of jumping in. Particularly the idea of signing a check that was bigger than the entire annual turnover of the company.

My advisor succeeded, through a combination of moral support and innate professionalism, to get both the Banque Populaire de Bourgogne and the Société Générale on board. Finally, Crédit Agricole also confirmed it was willing to lend me funds. I had what I needed–I just had to sign on the dotted line.

There is a saying that goes, "nothing ventured, nothing gained". I am here to tell you that it is true. Certainly there were sleepless nights and self-doubt along the way. But my mind was made up, and the challenge gave me the chance to know myself better, to once again push my limits and take on another adventure. As a result, today we run a successful business dedicated to great food and wine with a restaurant, hotel, artisan shops and 1,000 hectares of *garrigue*, all in celebration of the *art de vivre* of the Mediterranean lifestyle.

Jacques Ribourel had totally renovated L'Hospitalet–an estate that dated back to 1561–giving it back a harmony and geometric precision. But it still needed a soul, and that was the challenge that we set ourselves. L'Hospitalet became the natural base for developing the business. Its location in the Clape Massif, in the heart of Narbonne's national park, was inspirational. We were surrounded by the native animals, plants and wildlife of our region. To come across rare wild orchids growing in this exceptional limestone *terroir* was a lesson in the beauty of the world. The quality of the wines rapidly grew beyond my wildest expectations.

Our sales grew inexorably and in four years the turnover had doubled and the shape and ambition of the company changed. Our gamble had paid off. The banks were happy and I was sleeping better. I was able to buy other properties that allowed me to discover new *terroirs*, new grape varieties and continue to uncover the staggering diversity and potential of the Languedoc. In 2006, I bought Domaine de l'Aigle near Limoux, a site perfectly adapted to great chardonnay and pinot noir. Its high altitude meant that these traditional Burgundy varieties thrived. In 2009, we increased the quality potential of our Corbières wines with the purchase of Château Aigues-Vives in Boutenac from Bordeaux's Dourthe family. In 2011, I fell in love with the natural beauty and biodiversity around Château La Sauvageonne in the Terrasses du Larzac appellation close to Montpellier. It was formerly owned by Fred Brown, a cultured Englishman who had already begun an extensive replanting and renovation program. A villa stood sentinel over the vineyards at the top of a huge schist hillside, and all that was left for me to do was to renovate the cellars and share these "*paysage*" wines[1] with our distributors.

In 2012, the bishop and winemaker Monseigneur Bertrand de La Soujeole asked me to take over his eponymous estate so he could concentrate on his religious life. The Malepère appellation became another string on our bow, as this terroir is the kingdom of cabernet franc in the South of France. I adore the structure, finesse and typicity of this grape, and when blended with malbec it can reveal a whole new side to its personality.

At the same time we acquired Château les Karantes in a valley just outside Narbonne-Plage overlooking the sea. We were asked to do so by the American Knsyz family and happily agreed, deepening our presence and commitment in La Clape.

With all of this, in 15 years, we had gone from 60 hectares to over 550 hectares.

Being a successful vineyard owner means having the courage of your convictions and mastering your own destiny. Without these two things, you cannot even hope to make truly great wines. That is the belief I have lived by.

1. "*Paysage*" wines: journalist and writer Pierre Casamayor's words for indicating the beauty of specific terroirs.

I have learnt to feel, read and communicate with my vineyards. A visceral link between us has somehow always been there, something that goes way beyond what I can touch and see. I was lucky enough to have been born in an environment where I was encouraged to practice both rugby and vine growing, and where priorities were set by the seasons. Today, the second true passion of my life has become the all-encompassing one. Unlike rugby, you can play it for longer, although there are still risks involved.

These years of buying up vines strengthened the diversity of our offer, while regular traveling helped me better understand markets and distribution chains in France and overseas. Progress is always slow and you have to fight to be accepted by buyers and consumers. I was helped by my experiences in rugby, by my refusal to give up and by my obsession with working hard–as well as a few lucky meetings along the way. At the same time our team was strengthened by generous, exacting, courageous people who shared our values and were not afraid to lead.

Over the past 10 years, we have taken our philosophy to over 100 countries, while still holding true to the values of southern France.

6

The *Art de Vivre* of the South

We needed to reinforce our shared identity. This was the subject of a seminar held for the board of directors with our English vice-president Peter Darbyshire, who had worked in numerous roles across the world of wine and spirits. He, working with his friend James Guillepain from Champagne, helped us to understand what consumers were looking for and how to develop a new strategy for reaching them.

It has to be said that some French companies are not particularly adept at remembering that 99 percent of their clients are normal consumers and only 1 percent are experts. To reach the majority you need to understand what they want without sacrificing your roots or convictions. Not an easy task. To get the ball rolling, we set out our shared vocabulary. Our different ranges of wines were separated and ranked by category: variety-led, *terroir*-led, sparkling, *vins doux naturels*; and by theme: organic, biodynamic, no-added sulphur. These themes became the bedrock of the company. We were committed to environmental values and did everything we could to ensure the vineyards we left behind would be healthy for future generations by farming them biodynamically. We had 350 hectares already converted to this method, making us among the most prolific biodynamic farmers in the world. At the same time, our brand Autrement became the leading organic wine in the French market.

Innovation has always been an essential part of our DNA. We created the category of "no-added sulphur" wines by launching the brand Naturae, largely in France and North America. It remains a niche market for now but we believe it will see the same growth as organic wines in the future.

Our next target was to team up with other local producers to promote the concept of "South of France" wines to an international audience.

My friend Jacques Michaud, a law professor in Montpellier, has always championed this region. He believed that the link between the Languedoc and the Roussillon should be strengthened by bringing back the term Septimanie, which was the name of a French province in the 7th century whose geographic boundaries almost exactly mirror the region today. His idea was visionary, and quickly received the endorsement of Georges Frêche, president of the region. Frêche, a cultural powerhouse and talented orator, tried but failed to sell the idea to Catalonia. Not about to give up, he decided to find a new concept. He asked me to be part of the conversation. We kept returning to the idea of the South of France and finally were all in agreement. The concept was officially christened on the steps of the Narbonne town hall, a former bishop's palace. Frêche roused the fervour of the crowd with the words, "People of the South, stand up! This is your territory, your identity!" Six hundred people stood up on that early summer day and broke into applause. We then launched an ambitious marketing campaign, which had the built-in advantage that no matter where we went, people would immediately understand where we were from. We had successfully found our place between Bordeaux in southwest France and Provence in the southeast. Our region had given us a heritage, a keen sense of pride and deep roots. We now wanted to share those along with our abilities and our wines–a challenge that we gave ourselves 10 years to achieve.

The South of France region has blindingly beautiful assets, namely its size, open spaces and diversity. Preserving these assets while allowing a moderate and intelligent growth of its towns and cities was also a key part of our strategy, as we know the Mediterranean is increasingly prized as a place to live and visit.

Our motto "the *art de vivre* of wines from the South" takes on all its resonance and meaning.

It is a lifestyle that is based on the symbolism of the Mediterranean Sea–welcoming, warming, linking us to our Italian and Spanish neighbours, and farther to the south to Maghreb and the Near East. The origins of our monotheistic religion lie on her shores, with all the nations around her sharing a common link back to the founding father Abraham, the link between Christianity, Judaism and Islam, the cradle of humanist values spread by the voyages of the Greeks and Romans. It is a fine heritage, one that favours the opening of hearts and offering a welcoming hand to build a better future for the generations to come.

One of our initiatives was the creation of a Confrérie des Chevaliers de l'Art de Vivre, as a way of spreading our heritage, identity and customs. For one week at the beginning of each spring, we receive visitors from all over the world who celebrate the best of the Mediterranean right alongside us.

Our *art de vivre* has another happy result thanks to the local vines, olive oil, honey and abundant local produce. American medical professionals, who have noted the health benefits associated our lifestyle, call it the French Mediterranean Paradox. So how are we able to live better, longer and in more robust health, without sacrificing ambition and excellence? We believe the answer lies partly in the values of love, community and tolerance communicated through our bottles of wine, each one in turn a reflection of the diversity of our *terroirs*.

Local chefs played their own formidable part in spreading the word, contributing to the generosity of spirit on the plate and far beyond.

The original sense of the phrase *art de vivre* was growing stronger before our eyes–the art of living, the idea of life being elevated to a work of art, that most profound and potent symbol of human achievement, the trace of God's grace in all of us.

We try to be both dreamers and realists: tomorrow is the start of a new era, where the awakening of consciousness can plant the seeds for a future where we can live happily in peace and benefit from the riches of creation. We simply have to find new ways of learning.

The art of living is also the art of appreciating music. It is impossible to live in a world without music because even silence makes room for the harmonious sounds of nature; birds singing, the rustle of the wind, the cries of animals, the whispering of the stars in the early morning light–all sounds that can be seen as the breath of God, the faraway echo of the Big Bang that brought us into existence many billions of years ago.

We set up an art gallery at Château L'Hospitalet as a place for local artists to exhibit their works and for a yearly celebration of a major national or international artist. Rodin's bronzes, Jean-Pierre Rives's sculptures and the brilliant exhibition of Yann Arthus-Bertrand's *La Terre Vue du Ciel* photographs have all attracted crowds and focused attention on what we are doing here.

We drew our inspiration and our energy from the inexhaustible source of the southern *art de vivre*, and found ourselves in harmony with its poetry and gentle way of life.

Launching a music festival seemed the natural next step, and my love of jazz did the rest...

7

Jazz at L'Hospitalet

Our jazz festival launched in 2004. It was not easy at first, and it took four years before these summer evenings started to attract attention and critical acclaim.

Preparing the whole thing from beginning to end was pretty challenging for my team, but they put together a top-level program and have built on it since with a wide variety of artists. It has become an annual institution. Artists play in the château's central courtyard surrounded–and inspired–by vines. We've received moving feedback over the years from Yuri Buenaventura; Maceo Parker; Earth, Wind and Fire; Kid Creole; Kool and the Gang; Liz McComb; the Golden Gate Quartet; Michel Jonasz...

Jazz is to music what *terroir* is to wine. It speaks to the soul, to the depth of our being and our roots. Jazz exists in different forms, just as wine comes from an infinite variety of grapes and regions. Each vintage, even issued from the same patch of earth, will be different from the next–either subtly or profoundly–like each improvisation and each musician adds an extra and entirely new shade and tonality to the music. I love the positive energy of jazz; it restores and elevates my spirits. And I love how there are endless varieties of this style of music and that everyone can find one that speaks to them.

Each year, the blending of different styles brings a super-charged atmosphere and heightened emotions. After the main show, local groups take over the jazz cellar and music continues into the early hours. And to kick things off in the right spirit, every night our chef prepares magnificent platters of local Mediterranean food matched to our best wines.

July 5, 2004

Dominique Rieux and his band are setting up on the stage in the middle of the courtyard. There are around 30 of us waiting for the first evening to get underway. I barely remember the concert itself, but it is cold, and the only spectators are my family and a few friends. At the end of the concert, I say to my wife, "Next year, we'll do better".

Beginnings are never easy. You have to keep the flame alive while the dream becomes a reality. Success is usually little more than sticking something out.

The first three years are fairly similar, but little by little we manage to stoke up a sense of energy and a loyal and growing group comes along and joins in.

August 2007

Five hundred seats are crammed into the courtyard of L'Hospitalet, leaving just enough space to walk around the outside. Most of the spectators have already eaten in the park that stretches out behind the pool.

That night, on a stage set against the building's façade, Yuri Buenaventura sings his version of *Ne Me Quitte Pas* with his South American accent and his piercingly clear voice. At the end of the song, he stops the concert for several minutes and begins to talk to the audience about what he is feeling right here and now. In a few words he reveals how he had travelled from Colombia to study at the Sorbonne, sharing some of his most personal insights and experiences with us. He speaks of the vibrations he feels in this place, of the significance of sharing music, food, wine, a starry night and the scent of lavender. I am overcome with emotion, a lump in my throat, close to tears. Not only is he expressing himself beautifully, but he has perfectly encapsulated the spirit of L'Hospitalet. I am far from alone in this response: all around me, the audience starts drawing together in a sort of shared communion.

August 6, 2010

Maceo Parker is playing. The central courtyard is packed. One of the world's most famous jazz saxophonists, who has toured with James Brown, is here playing with his band. The atmosphere is electric and the energy that the musicians are giving off is all-enveloping. Parker is riffing off the audience, playing snippets from his anthology, including a 20-minute solo, at the end of which he turns to his backing singers and raises his hands to the sky as a gesture of thanks to his mentor. He plays for two hours 45 minutes and makes us jump for joy.

August 8, 2010

Michel Legrand, one of the world's great musicians, is to launch his new show after Nathalie Dessay has played her set. This is a world première. I arrive at 7pm and, for some unknown reason, feel nervous. Ten minutes later, one of my team announces that Michel Legrand wants to cancel the first part of the show. His agent hadn't told him the scheduling details and he doesn't want to go on at 11pm. I go to meet him and his charming wife, and sense immediately that there is another reason for his annoyance. Everyone is feeling the pressure; Nathalie Dessay has just arrived from Japan and the afternoon rehearsal has not gone well. In the end my friend Jeff Senegas takes care of the first part of the show, and the two French stars perform an excellent set.

August 2011

China Moses has the audience in the palm of his hand for the show opener with his voice, his rhythm and his hypnotic hip-swaying. Next up, the group Incognito comes on stage, arriving straight from London. We get lost in their musical universe. After 20 minutes it starts raining and we have to stop the show for security reasons. I ask the crowd to be patient but some go home. Half an hour later, the musicians choose to continue with an acoustic set in the restaurant. And so begins one of the greatest moments of the decade of concerts. A jamming session–*un bœuf* in French–watched by the 400 people who have stayed behind, standing on chairs or sitting on the bar, spectators and musicians all together. The atmosphere is incredible, just pure happiness.

August 2013

The prince of *La Boîte de jazz* is playing with his band. It is the second time that Michel Jonasz has appeared at the festival, and he gives us an incredible two-hour set. The public loves both his music and his warm stage presence. He is accompanied by René Coll and his orchestra, a fellow Languedocian who was born in Trèbes near Carcassonne.

August 1, 2014, 8.15pm

In the park, around 1,200 visitors have settled down to eat. The skies overhead look menacing. Boy George is playing and he is getting concerned about the weather. We manage to install a waterproof canvas over the stage. Right on cue, it starts to rain. I take over the microphone and tell the audience that a touch of rain is good for the vines, that they are drops from God. We hand out clear plastic ponchos and settle back to enjoy a rain-sodden evening. Happily the skies clear up after 20 minutes and an hour later everyone is enjoying a spectacular show. Boy George shares his memories, the excesses of his past and his new life filled with love and spirituality. He sings his song *Hare Krishna,* dedicated to his Hindu beliefs, and tears of joy roll down his face. Arms open, the singer and his musicians thank Providence. We feel the beating of an angel's wings.

August 2, 2014, 7.45pm

My friend Yuri Buenaventura, king of salsa and godfather of the festival, comes over to me. He asks how things are going. This is the last concert and he needs to take the pulse of things to share it with his musicians and get them fired up. I tell him that apart from one or two small things, we are likely to see one of our greatest years. I don't tell him that the upcoming weather forecast isn't so great, but I am hoping that we will be spared the worst. And we have a surprise planned for the end of the show, at 10.23pm precisely–an air display with the Breitling Jet Team.

At 10.10pm, I head over to the organiser who tells me that the clouds are too heavy and that he will have to cancel the planes. I ask him to pass me the radio so I could speak directly to the captain, my friend Jacques Bothelin, an adventurer and champion pilot. I say, "Jacques, you have to get here! Can you take off from Béziers and tell me how it looks over here when you arrive?" He replies, "Gérard, give me 10 minutes".

It is 10.20pm. In the park, it is raining lightly. Like the night before, the audience is discovering the joy of eating under the rain, almost as glamorous as Gene Kelly's *Singing in the Rain*. I took to the stage to tell them, "I have some good news for you; the Breitling Jet Team are about to make a visit". Three minutes later, right on time, the jets pass overhead and the crowd bursts into applause. As if by magic the rain stops and the skies clear. The air show lasts 20 minutes and during the whole thing I can feel the energy vibrating from the spectators. Yuri Buenaventura is reassured: he knows now that he can simply harness the energy that is flowing around the courtyard. He shares the rhythms of his Latin music with us for the next two hours, turning the entire place into one big dance floor.

Moments like this remind us that life is for living and that music breaks down barriers and borders. All artists, even the biggest stars, are above all fellow human beings who use their voices, and their warmth, to share their world with us.

Discovering new landscapes and pushing limits is our philosophy for life. The success of this festival, now attended by 6,000 people over the course of four days, makes real our commitment to excellence. We also get to share the experience with friends and clients whom we hope in turn become our ambassadors.

8

The Human Adventure

The human adventure of our group is based on the coming together of passionate men and women who are altruistic, courageous and want to share the values of the Mediterranean lifestyle.

The years spent on the rugby pitch gave me a specific view of management, one where individual success should always be for the benefit of the team, and where leadership should be best expressed through mutual respect. To my mind, self-discipline means ensuring a level playing field and playing by the rules.

The emotional dimension is also very important. In a family company, and particularly within the wine industry, there are not only great years. Our success and financial results are dependent in many ways on the reputation of specific vintages and the quantity of wine produced in each one. It is critical to not just focus on short-term success but to be in for the long-haul with goals set over at least five-year intervals, allowing each team member to approach their work with ambition and confidence. The life of a wine company is necessarily guided by the seasons, the changing climate and the generosity and capriciousness of nature. It is essential that everyone who works in the company understands this and is ready to work together. Doing so, I sincerely believe, gives us the chance to find a deeper meaning in life.

To allow people to grow, continuous training is necessary, as is developing a set of shared values and references, and understanding that each action has a symbolic as well as a practical dimension.

Each December we celebrate the act of pruning the vines with a festival to coincide with the launch of the year's sales campaign. Each new year in the vineyard starts with pruning. This action of cutting away unnecessary branches to increase power and vigour in the ones left behind is repeated five times throughout the year. It is essential for the quality of the grapes that will eventually grow, and pruners are key members of the team. Out there in the cold and the wind, for up to eight hours a day, takes endurance, stubbornness, and commitment, but also skill, precision and love for a job well done.

A plant, and particularly an old vine, deserves respect and all the consideration due to its age and the quality of the fruit that it produces. It needs to be loved and cherished. Making sure that is done correctly is part of the overall plan that I have followed over the past few years ensuring a holistic treatment for everyone who works with us, and by extension our vines.

The arrival of Richard Planas in 2002 was a turning point in our development of precision agriculture. He was brought in as estate director to manage the team and introduce a training program and identity charter. It was not easy at first to change people's habits, to channel their energies and open their spirits, but he achieved it through diplomacy and by having the courage of his convictions.

After a year, the key team members understood the value of sharing and exchanging ideas. Any clashes of egos had subsided. We had succeeded in creating a meticulous plan for running our properties, treating each one individually, plot by plot.

Once the first phase was underway, Cédric Lecareux got going with the next step; namely instilling good daily practices in not just the new team members but in all of us, making certain that the corporate culture was adhered to in all departments, from the offices to the cellars. Cédric also brought us his organisational skills, his rigour and his excellent ability to communicate.

We spent time ensuring the teams visited all our estates to challenge any assumptions that may have grown stale and to uncover potential areas for improvement. For this, we nominated Ghislain Coux to work as cellar master across all properties, so he could follow details such as harvest dates, vinification methods, aging and bottling.

Blending, which takes place between January and March, is a key time in the elaboration of a great wine. The blend itself is shaped by the character of the vintage and the specificities of the product that, year after year, must be true to the *terroir* as well as the beliefs of the person behind the wine. Learning how to do this takes time. I saw how patient my father was with his colleagues, and I learnt to be the same. Effective blending is the fruit of teamwork.

My father taught me so much about the basics of this profession, not least the art of blending. It is a skill that requires both restraint and preparation. A morning of hard work that is best prepared for by a light meal the night before and a good night's sleep, followed by a full breakfast to make sure you are ready to go.

Memories of past tastings echo around the room, just as the walls of a church whisper the thousands of prayers that have been offered there. The memories held here transmit a positive energy. Personally I like to taste in a room that is kept at 18°C and to serve the wines, whether red, rosé or white, at 15°C. The order of the tasting is always the same. We turn off our telephones, close the door and start by laying out the objectives of the session and talking about any recent changes in the cellar.

When all that is done, we get underway.

Ensuring a good relationship with the technical director and the cellar master is key–tasting alone is just never as effective.

My greatest level of trust is reserved for Jean-Baptiste Terlay, our technical director, because he has to be the "guardian of the temple". He is the man who guarantees that our blends are of the highest quality, every time.

Finding balance and being sure that the blend results in a wine that is true to itself involves the careful use of all five senses. This is where we enter into the realm of emotions and intuition. You need to be aligned, in tune with the spirit of the wine. Sometimes you need four or five tasting sessions to get to the right result. You get there by application, discipline, and rigour, but also by simply feeling, talking and sharing impressions, each time inching closer towards the Holy Grail–a wine that is in harmony with the terroir that it came from, and expresses its own individual character and its particular vintage.

Meeting Jean-Claude Berrouet was a key moment. In August 1989, I went to a conference on barrel aging given by the Château Petrus winemaker at Château Notre-Dame-de-Gaussan, an estate just a few miles away. After a fascinating two-hour discussion on the effects of barrel aging on wines, I approached him to ask a question. To my great surprise, he turned out to be a rugby fan and recognised me, and asked me to visit him in Libourne.

Without waiting for a second invitation, I headed up to Libourne in January 1990, taking with me samples of my latest vintage of Domaine de Villemajou. It was not just his simplicity and kindness that astounded me, but also his incredible talent. Without fail, over the last 20 years, we have spent a day together every year, working in his laboratory, tasting and working on a wine blend. Jean-Claude, the man who has himself vinified 50 vintages of Petrus, but was also the winemaker of La Fleur-Petrus, Trotanoy, and Magdeleine, became my reference, my guide. He opened my eyes to the true meaning of perfect balance between the left and right brain–the true meaning of how to balance analysis and intuition.

He also taught me that wine carries its own message, its own music, that it reveals the soils that it came from, its grape varieties and the character of its owner. What is necessary is to find the essential truth of a wine, without artifice or unnecessary additions, by pinpointing its origins. He taught me that tasting is not just a simple, quick task, but one that you must take your time over and feel the vibrations, structure, texture and backbone of a wine.

Jean-Claude also taught me the importance of paying attention to the tiniest details, from handling glasses and test tubes with the utmost delicacy to the precise methodology with which he prepared the tastings. Nothing was left to chance. We have continued, at regular intervals, to exchange and taste together, and they are always enriching, intense experiences.

In 1988, a few days after I officially began my wine career, I asked the regional delegate Marc Dubernet to visit me and give his opinion of my cellars. His advice was precious, even if I was sometimes defensive; perhaps because the early loss of my father was still fresh and painful.

Marc gently reminded me that he had spent 20 years with my father building up a sizeable cooperative wine cellar. He is naturally a talented mathematician, skilled at shaping information and at practical application of knowledge. I am more direct, intuitive and less rational. It took me a few years to really listen to his advice, but ever since, we have reached a high level of mutual trust, each able to draw the best out of the other. He is an exceptional man, able to analyse and summarise situations quickly but always with great modesty. Our judgments are almost always complementary–there is no ego in our relationship, and it is a true joy to work together on achieving quality for the everyday wines just as much as for the fine wines.

I must also pay my respects to Olivier Roux and his team for the production side of the wines; selecting the best corks and the most beautiful bottles. We have just invested in an ultramodern cellar in the middle of the vines. This environmentally sound cellar, in the shape of an H, represents the future of our group, our ultimate guarantee to the consumer that every detail is being taken care of right up to bottling. Paul Correia and his team provide the quality control. It is not only the taste of the wine that is important here, but also the fail-safe respect for the procedures.

When I was 18 I was shy and introverted. To help me grow into myself, my father decided to send me out on the road, over the summer months, to sell Blanquette de Limoux to cooperative cellars around the region. I might as well have been selling ice to Eskimos. It was a baptism by fire. I spent my first three days barely daring to even go in to see anyone. Luckily, I met a kind director at the wine cooperative in Villeveyrac who could tell how nervous I was, and he built up my confidence by immediately placing an order for 300 bottles. I walked out of the meeting happy and proud, practically bounding into the car park. I never looked back. Over the next two months, I sold 20,000 bottles and flooded the region with my bubbles. Warning that I wouldn't be back, I recommended to my clients that they should stock up early for the Christmas rush.

I have always considered sales as the heart of what we do, and I have huge respect for anyone who can fill out an order book and keep the rest of the team in employment. Sales, at its heart, is like a sports match. You can win or you can lose, but it is always a negotiation. You need to be mentally prepared before you arrive, with your arguments sharpened, your priorities in order so that you and the client can both find a way to create a long-term partnership. It is less difficult nowadays, as our wines are known and recognised for their quality. But the pressure remains. To do this job, you need to be an adrenaline junkie.

Éric Lacombe worked hard to ensure that the sales team who were dealing with supermarkets were also on point, once again underlining the fact that our shared values are our great strength. Stéphane Durand, my ex-Narbonne teammate, joined us to develop sales in restaurants and independent wine shops across France. His enthusiasm, passion and energy were infectious. Éric, Stéphane and alongside them, Patrick Costes, Stéphane Jollec, Aurélien Casteran, Romain Jammes, Cyril Jaffro and Philippe Folch do an amazing job of sharing our approach to life with their clients. They are not my colleagues but my brothers in arms. I am lucky enough to be surrounded by people with heart and courage and who can fight the good fight. My cousin Guy Bertrand, who started out working alongside my father, perfectly encapsulates the union between the two generations.

When selling overseas, the complexity and diversity of different markets make things even more difficult. Alistaire Pine oversees the American team with passion and a sense of adventure. Alexandra Ladeuil is in charge of Europe, helped by Laura Garrigue and Suzie Thevenin; Jan Visser in Asia, Jean-Philippe Turgeon in Canada and Christophe Balay manages the duty-free markets. All do a wonderful job of harnessing the different personalities of our distributors and sharing our methods and values, while still remaining respectful to the different culture of each country. Our approach is tailored to each one.

Our growing size made it necessary to create a marketing division; a skill that is far more difficult than it can at first appear. It was essential to back up my intuitions with strategic studies and research, and I handed the department over to someone who would work independently and with a very different approach from my own. Karine Hamelin and her team look after the marketing with professionalism, panache and sincerity.

Sharing our knowledge and know-how is not just about having a communication strategy externally in France and beyond, but also within our own company. Véronique Braun, working with Katia Daguet and her colleagues, ensure we are on point with journalists, opinion leaders and wine lovers while keeping track of all mentions of our brands across the written press, radio, television, internet and social networks. She also takes care of our restaurant–aptly named L'Art de Vivre–and our hotel, the artisan gallery and all the events that we hold throughout the year.

I met my right-hand man Michael Van Duijn three years ago. His domain is the back office, or in other words the staff and the office processes while I am the front office, looking after client relations and the quality of our wines. Each role is essential, and our relationship is founded on mutual respect and a permanent open communication. His Flemish origins give him keen organisational skills, and his role as managing director gives me the freedom to look more globally at our endeavours, certain in the knowledge that he has things in hand, such as the building of our new cellars, which he oversaw from start to finish.

9

Getting to the Heart of Things

On the journey of self-discovery, you must first take a step towards others. It means learning how to cope with stress, self-doubt and facing the future and the opportunities that it offers with confidence. By doing so, you can move beyond the judgement and criticisms of those around you. To be at one with the spirit of the world means undertaking an internal journey–something that I learnt very early in life, helped without doubt by the death of my father.

Rugby gave me the chance to transcend myself and to push my limits. Sport also gave me self-confidence and belief in my teammates. This brotherhood has gladdened my heart, opened my eyes and guided me ever since, because once the light of understanding switches on, it is never extinguished.

In wine, as in rugby, faith gives you the necessary courage to go out, discover what is necessary and get on with achieving it.

From the age of 22, I instinctively knew that my professional life would involve traveling and meeting all types of people. I first built, with the help of several loyal ambassadors, a solid network in France, then set out to take my first steps in Europe, Asia and then North America. It took me 20 years to understand the subtleties of the global markets. The Anglo-Saxons were the first to understand the potential of French *terroirs*, and to welcome our wines into their homes, led by the wines of Bordeaux that were shaped by their links to England. But the category of South of France wines was still limited to France, barely known outside our borders. This reality simply reinforced my conviction that there was no point relying solely on the quality of the wines. We needed to go further and establish strong relations with distributors who shared our values and our way of life.

The competitive spirit that had been forged by rugby was my main ally, because the first few years were tough and at times seemed almost impossible. I understood why it was so difficult for my father to sell his first bottles. I was determined not to give up or give in, even if doubts and sleepless nights became constant companions for a while.

Eventually I had a few lucky meetings, and found strong personalities who gave me their trust and opened their networks to me. Momentum grew, a feeling of shared purpose–often helped by enjoyable evenings sharing food and wine together in ways that echoed those wonderful post-match rugby celebrations. When the barriers fall and we find shared ground with someone, we know what it is to be human, to share what is essential. The world of wine opens the hearts of men, gives them courage, empathy and common ground. To share a few good bottles is also to open the door to getting to know one another, to leave our egos behind and build something lasting.

Régis Boucabeille, originally from Canet-d'Aude near Narbonne but now based out of Brussels, was one of the first to promote the wines of the Languedoc-Roussillon across Europe. He is a courageous, energetic man with a rare sense of conviction. He was very kind to me, and helped to open up several key markets such as Belgium, Holland, Germany and the Nordic countries. He was the first ambassador for my wines on an international stage and showed me the art of negotiation and how to read different markets.

One winter evening, we spent three hours trying to convince a buyer of the quality of our Castelmaure wines–a beautiful region in the hills of Corbières where my father had done much to raise quality. Clearly, whatever we were saying wasn't working. Then Régis had a genius idea. "My dear sir", he said, "we can't leave here without at least tasting the wines, the winemakers deserve at least that. As it is late, how about we taste them over a meal at the restaurant next door?" We made our way through all the bottles and, at two in the morning in the corner of the bar, on a scrap of paper, the buyer agreed to purchase 30,000 more. You don't learn these techniques in school. You can only learn them on the pitch.

Hervé Robert, a Frenchman based out of Düsseldorf, helped me understand how to read clients' buying patterns and to supply what they need. He developed an exceptional sales technique with Jacques Wein Depot and became adept at sharing, with Kathy Feron and her team, the French lifestyle with German consumers. A *tour de force*!

In the United States, Mel Dick welcomed me warmly. An extraordinary man with the trust and backing of the Chaplin family, he had created–over the course of 40 years–the biggest wine and spirits distribution company in America. He began his life in Brooklyn, where he was childhood friends with the great American boxer Sugar Ray Robinson, giving us a common set of values found in combat sports such as boxing and rugby. He offered me a chance in New York and said, "Gérard, if you make a success of things here, come back to me and we'll talk about getting you into the other states". In six months, I had been back and forth six times to Manhattan and its surrounding areas to sell my first bottles. Momentum grew, and as promised he introduced me to his team and I found myself with seven people to represent us in the States.

In 25 years, we have created an international network based on our essential values of communication and altruism, and we are now present in over 100 countries, flying the flag for our region.

For the past 10 years, we have partnered with some of the greatest chefs in the world–something that has given me the chance to try out local foods in the world's best restaurants. We are hugely proud to have created links between so many different cultures, and to have matched so many wonderful dishes with the wines of southern France.

Our country, history and *art de vivre* are loved the world over. We need to continue to cultivate that spirit, the French flair that can be so seductive, while remaining open and respectful of all other traditions.

After so many years, I still enjoy traveling, discovering new cultures and landscapes alongside the traditions, customs and rituals of each country. And I have learnt how being French is a wonderful passport. Traveling makes you more tolerant, more conscious and receptive to other points of view. My many stays in Japan have allowed me to better understand this country. I have always been impressed by the solidarity of spirit and the force of the Japanese people after the tragedy of Fukushima.

From Tokyo to New York via Amsterdam, Brussels, Miami, Kuala Lumpur, Rio de Janeiro, Shanghai, London, Berlin, Mexico City and Sydney, I love to feel the energy of these cities and to discover the magic within them.

Traveling the world also means being impatient to return home and to connect once again with the spirit of your own land, your terroir and your ancestors. Each time I return to my family in Corbières, I feel my heart quicken and I am overcome by the beauty of this place, the memories that it holds. By coming home, I once again feel connected to my deepest self.

10

The Pyramid of the Senses

Wine is a multi-faceted substance, far more complicated than a simple product or drink. For five thousand years or more, it has been the constant companion of man, the link between successive civilisations. As a symbol of the blood of Christ, the Catholic Church sees in wine a sign of unity. An understanding of its history, of what it has meant to different societies over the years, is hugely enlightening.

Until the end of the 19th century, wine was the traditional drink of certain European countries: France, Italy, Spain, Portugal; and then later Switzerland, Austria and Eastern European countries such as Crimea and Georgia–the historic cradle of European wine, still making excellent reds today–together with the Tokaj region of Hungary and Romania, where some equally excellent sweet wines are produced. Still later, wine was cultivated in Chile, Argentina and Mexico, building momentum in recent years as part of a great wave of globalisation. California saw its first vineyards planted by Spanish monks and is now a global powerhouse, contributing strongly to the growth of wine consumption in the United States.

More recently still, Asia (first Japan then China) has developed an interest in wine. Not only for its taste but also its culture and history, and for the prestige of certain French wines, most notably those from Bordeaux and Burgundy. With respect, ceremony and humility, the Japanese favoured French wines, then European and then those of the New World, placing the product at the centre of their culinary traditions. Their ancestral cooking is based around fish, which is not always considered ideal for the red wines that they prefer. Over the decades, they began to slowly introduce wine to their gala dinners with great refinement, a mark of cultural exchange. The annual consumption per head remains relatively small, yet wine is essential during certain celebrations such as New Year's.

In China, the swift growth of the economy at the end of the 1980s meant thousands of newly created millionaires and an emerging middle class for whom wine–and most notably the classified growths of Bordeaux–became a status symbol. To be part of this closed circle of Pétrus, Latour and Lafite Rothschild collectors meant a passport to the global elite.

To the west of China, Russia developed a similar consumer culture, linked to a global phenomenon of luxury brands in *haute couture*, ready-to-wear collections and jewellery. This world is run according to remarkably well-orchestrated fashion weeks, walking circuses reserved for the financial elite of the planet but rolled-out alongside an astute strategy of mass-market. Wine became part of this frenetic dance of consumerism.

The traditional *en primeurs* tasting in Bordeaux is today far from the only ritual dedicated to unveiling the quality of the latest vintage. Certainly the power and structure of the Bordeaux marketplace continues to give it an advantage, but on all five continents there has been an explosion of trade fairs and tastings that are not just for professionals but for consumers and wine lovers. Social networks and the multitude of apps that we can download to our phones and tablets mean that access to information about these events is available to everyone.

In the 1980s, French, English and American journalists were among the first to grow the profession of wine tasting; the first two in an academic and often encyclopedic manner, the latter a little more innovative. After falling in love with France, Robert Parker had a genius idea to publish a newsletter, *The Wine Advocate*, in which he would rank wines while breaking with the traditional European marking system of scoring them on a scale of 0 to 20. He created the idea of ranking them out of a possible top score of 100. For many years, Parker was the palate of reference, and his global influence was as rapid as it was determinant for the hierarchy of wines. He created a level playing field between the Old and New World, and was blind to the power of established names. The elevation of Californian cabernet sauvignons to the same level as those from Bordeaux helped drive an increased interest in wine globally. We have moved, in 30 years, from a fairly limited market to a global one, where the rules change daily.

At the same time, labelling wines by grape variety, easier for new consumers to understand, has taken precedence over the mysteries of *terroir*. In the 1990s the Anglo-Saxons created a segmentation that was not simply based on the provenance of wines as had been typical in France, Italy or Spain (IGP: *indication géographique protégée*; or AOP: *Appellation d'origine protégée*), but a more pragmatic division into seven categories:

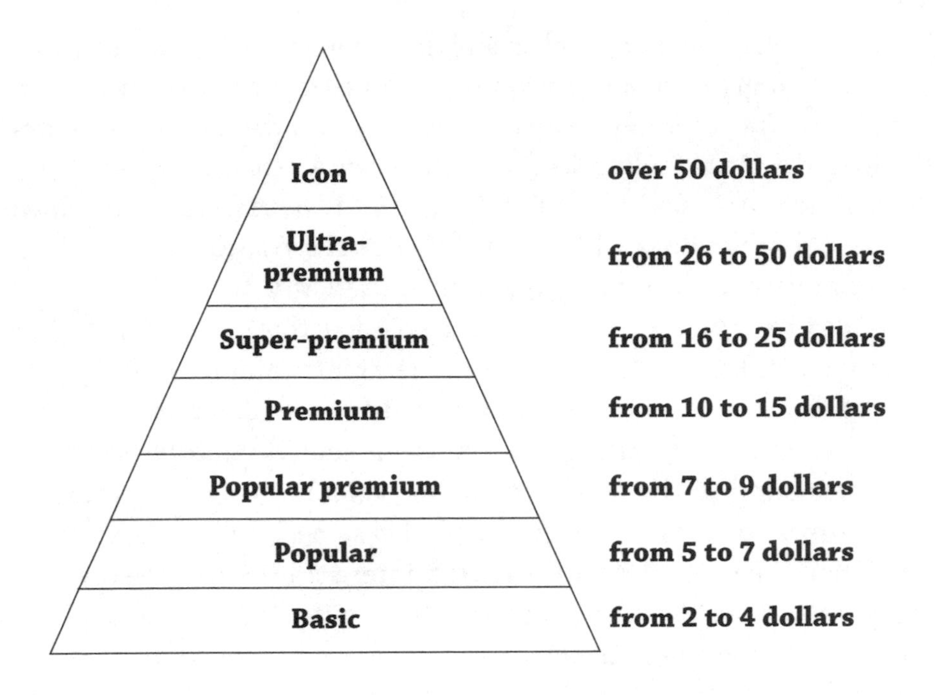

Today, after long reflection and plenty of practical experience, I believe it is time to organise a different hierarchy of wines, one that reflects that price is no longer the key criterion for consumers. Twenty years ago, the price ratio between a good-quality and an exceptional wine was at most tenfold. Today this difference has exploded to perhaps 100-fold. Interest in the grands crus wines grows ever stronger, and is often dependent on critics' reviews.

There is another new phenomenon linked to speculation and the production of limited-edition special *cuvées*, made in quantities too small to meet demand. At the same time, the financial crisis and the crackdown on corruption by the Chinese government have ensured that all is not smooth sailing. Demand has slowed–even if there remain certain reservoirs of growth such as Brazil, Nigeria, Colombia and India.

Another, more original, way to classify wines is by creating direct links not to the markets but to the experiences of those who drink them. Those who, little by little, are gaining in power and breaking free of the usual market rules. Wine lovers know that with little more than a few seconds and a mobile phone, they can connect directly to winemakers. There are no secrets anymore for those with a desire to learn. The planet has become a garden where the consumer, in his armchair while sipping a fine glass of rosé, can order pretty much anything he wants. There are of course logistical and shipping problems that limit this free exchange of information and goods, but it is undeniable that the consumer is gaining in power. Some have even become influential opinion leaders in the blogosphere.

For my part, I believe that a new, less commercially driven system will be propelled by the wants and needs of consumers, and will be divided into four main categories:

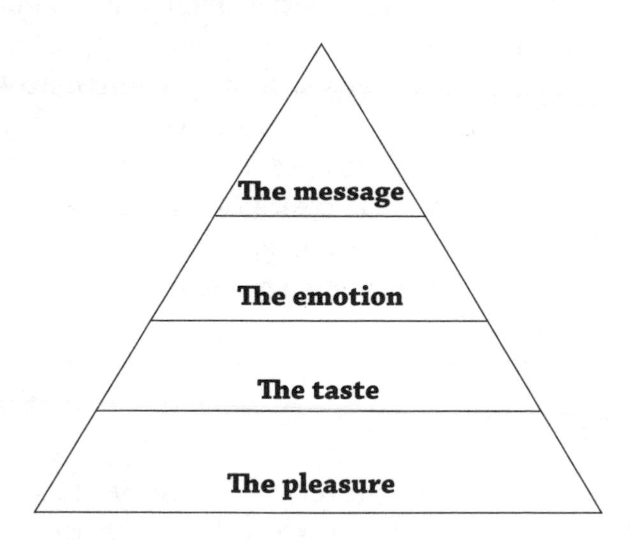

There are ever more people who are ready and willing to explore new horizons and open to an awakening of the senses. Men and women no longer need to be slaves to labels but can choose according to their own criteria and desires. We no longer drink wine as part of our daily "food for fuel" intake in the way that previous generations, whose jobs often involved hard physical labour, did. At the same time, the advances in vinification techniques, the willingness to leave grapes to ripen fully in the vineyard before harvest and dozens of other improvements in viticulture mean there has been an almost total elimination of faulty or bad bottles of wine.

Pleasure

The first level of wine appreciation is pleasure–an understanding that wine is a discovery to share. Today the number of people drinking wine every day continues to drop while the numbers of those who drink occasionally rises ever higher as we move toward a more sedentary lifestyle.

Pleasure in wine is characterised first of all by its colour: clear, brilliant, luminous. On the nose it should be intense and a reflection of the grape or blend of grapes that it comes from. Pleasure should be immediate. A wine is created to be drunk, not simply to taste, and a winemaker has succeeded only when at the end of a meal between friends, his bottle is empty.

Taste

This is a whole different universe. We are heading here to the famous "throat of happiness". Taste is found in the throat; it is what stays behind after you have taken a sip. It is possible here to distinguish between taste and aftertaste, something that wine professionals call *caudalie*. More typically we know it as "length"–

how long the taste of a wine remains in your mouth after you have finished your glass.

Generally taste is characterised by a sense of personality, an intensity and persistence that may be linked to older vines or to limited yields. It is fascinating, as you develop experience in tasting, to make the link between the taste of a wine and the intrinsic qualities of its *terroir*. The soil, subsoil and the immediate environment surrounding the vines impregnate the grape during its growth cycle, from May to September.

Grapes, after fermentation, are the only fruit able to deliver the myriad aromas of all other fruits and plants, as well as the characteristics of certain soil types (schist, iron, limestone). In comparison, cider tastes simply of apples.

As a true lover of food and wine, I love matching one with the other, particularly through studying recipes. The interaction of the two needs to be total, one building on the other through osmosis to create a symphony. Wine has an ability to amplify flavours and to enlarge what we understand by the terms sweet, salty, acidic and bitter. It contains endless other far more subtle notes related to how it is made and aged and the grapes that it comes from. It is an endless voyage of discovery, because taste is often a question of culture and tradition. The Japanese have discovered a "fifth taste" called *umami*. You can find it in certain dried fish or more simply in soy sauce. This finesse of appreciating taste exists in all cultures, even if the vocabulary used is not the same as our own.

Taste is the salt of life, and wine awakens its powers of seasoning.

Emotion

Now we are approaching the most essential thing: the heart.

Experiencing emotion through wines takes preparation. You must first of all surround yourself with people whom you love and appreciate. Next, the choice of wine should lend itself toward excellence, purity, truth, the alchemy between a winemaker and his *terroir*.

The vintage chosen should be at its peak, ready to drink. A great wine should begin to reveal its mysteries after 10 years in bottle, a great white or sparkling wine perhaps a little earlier. For *vins doux naturels*, I recommend at least 50 years of aging.

Having chosen the wine, give it a chance to be properly aerated by opening it a few hours early and decanting if necessary. The serving temperature is important. For all these details and the best food matches, I recommended following the advice of the winemaker, who has often written his suggestions on the back label, or those of a sommelier.

There are no absolute truths when it comes to matching food and wine, even if I generally recommend meat with red wine because the proteins will soften the tannins once in the mouth. With cheese, usually relatively acidic styles such as goat cheese are better with white wine, while softer textured cheeses are better with red. A strong cheese works best with sweet wines and *vins doux naturels*.

If all of these things come together, magic arrives. Time stops and you can simply be in the moment. Emotion is at its peak. The experience might be shared–all the guests around the table feeling the same opening of the spirit–or might sometimes be shared only among a few of you. Perhaps you may be the only one to have felt it, although if that is the case, the experience will be less strong, because shared emotion is the strongest kind.

In any case, I advise you before opening a great bottle of wine to choose your company well, because emotions such as these are rare and precious.

The message

After having woken to the possibilities of your five senses, it is possible to continue onwards to a new door; behind it lies the message.

Sometimes, the great flux of emotions leads to a mystical experience. You don't need faith to get there, but it certainly helps. If you reach the message, you will experience a feeling of inner peace, serenity, love and harmony. You are ready to commune with the spirit of the wine, to understand its very essence. Inevitably it takes time and practice to do this, along with a certain level of knowledge. But the most important thing is the capacity to be delighted.

Once it has happened, it becomes easier to recreate because we have allowed ourselves to grow. Jacob[1], in his dreams, saw a ladder linking heaven and earth, on which the angels of God were ascending and descending. Some wines have the potential to bring us this type of revelation, because they are unique unto themselves and the hands that crafted them were able to transmit the message of the *terroir*, the alchemy between soil, vineyard plot, grapes and vintage.

These rare wines are not the fruit of ego but of a perfect balance, where the humble hand of man can create a masterpiece, as with certain great painters. Here we approach the highest achievement of mankind: art.

Hallelujah!

1. The Bible Genesis 28:11-

11

Biodynamics

2002: Biodynamics is introduced at Cigalus

As a serious advocate of homeopathic medicine, I wanted to try out biodynamic farming on a few hectares of vines. I raised the topic with my passionate and committed vineyard manager Gilles de Baudus, who had learnt his trade under Jacques Mell, a board member at Demeter, the most important biodynamic organisation globally. We deliberately selected the most difficult, capricious vines that were not getting anywhere with conventional agriculture, to really get to the heart of whether this new method of farming would work. We divided a plot of four hectares into two equal halves–one half to farm biodynamically and the other using our usual approach of sustainable agriculture.

After two years of testing, we noticed a profound change in the biodynamic vines. The symptoms of fanleaf disease began to fade, as did the susceptibility of the merlot to suffer from poor fruit set. Instead the grapes were getting visibly more healthy and reaching a better ripeness.

We began to see such a success with the use of plant tinctures given in homeopathic doses and mixed with dynamised water[1] that we stopped using any chemical products.

1. Water is poured into a wooden vat, then dynamised by effecting left and right swirling motions for around 20 minutes, creating a vortex. The dynamisation

During the harvest, tasting the grapes was a surprisingly tactile pleasure. The taste was more intense and harmonious than usual, with a subtle tang from the products we had used.

The early results were equally encouraging in the cellar. Vinifying the two parts of the vineyard separately showed unequivocally that the biodynamic grapes had greater freshness, vitality of fruit and minerality. It brought home to me how unshakeable the link is between vines and the soils that nourish them.

It was clear that we had to convert the entire plot to biodynamics. This led to three or four years of purgatory, largely because of previous contamination of the soils. Everything comes from the earth and to the earth it must return!

Applying biodynamic products guided by the forces of the earth and the cosmos strengthened the harmony of our plantings. The influence of the moon, sun and stars during a plant's growth cycle is fundamental, particularly those inner planets and celestial bodies closer to the Sun (the moon, Mercury, Venus and Mars) and to a lesser extent the outer planets (such as Jupiter and Saturn).

Steiner wrote that, "the strong influence of the planets is transmitted to the plant through silicon and calcium carbonate". Silicon is a major component of the earth's crust–over 90 percent of it is made up of silicate minerals–and plays an essential role in the development of the plant. It transmits vitality, protects against disease, stimulates nutrient uptake and allows the plant to root itself more securely in its environment. Plants typically absorb bio-available silicon as a silicate, and its interaction with forests where trees grow closely together has long been observed. The part of the plant essential for

---

is created thanks to dynamic oscillation. Blades spinning in the water create a whirlpool that is continued for specific lengths of time depending on the type of biodynamic treatment that is being prepared. A motor will then cut the movement, creating a pause, before restarting in the opposite direction (the counter-whirlpool).

reproduction and the life cycle is linked to calcium carbonate, again through the influence of nearby planets.

The application of these principles in vine growing makes the influence of the earth and the heavens impossible to ignore–and this extends not just to making but to tasting wine.

My wise friend and advisor Jean-Claude Berrouet helped us understand the strange world of tasting stones. Sucking on pieces of rock, besides being a highly unusual way to pass an afternoon, reveals the taste of the *terroir* and has surprising similarities to tasting wine. Minerality is revealed through a tension that comes into play after a few moments, together with a mouth-watering quality. Limestone, for example, is salty. Round worn pebbles have the subtle taste of iron. It is a fascinating process and one that takes you back to childhood. How many times have you heard parents telling their children not to eat stones? In reality, what children are doing subconsciously is the most natural thing in the world; tasting minerals to feel close to nature. I've never seen a child actually swallow a stone.

Our fears are often responsible for breaking our connection with ancestral knowledge. Man committed the original sin through his desire for knowledge, forgetting that nature will always know more than we do, and that we are little more than travellers passing through. Nature has regulated life on this planet for billions of years, while the influence of man is very recent. When she is in danger, nature sends us warnings that we should listen to, and we should find a way to protect the earth from the aggressions of human overproduction.

The moon exerts a primordial influence on plants and in particular on vines. Ancient wisdom knew how to harness its power to guide the rhythm of work in vineyards and farms, which is why the lunar calendar should be the touchstone of all good organic or biodynamic winemakers.

It is important to make a distinction between these two methods of farming. Organic farming, indicated by the *Agriculture Biologique*, or AB, label in France, is already a significant advance on traditional methods of farming. It took hold as a widely followed practice around 30 years ago and led to the availability of high-quality wines, fruits, vegetables and hand-reared meats. Organic production guarantees healthy, natural products that taste good and have high nutritional value. As supermarkets as well as specialist outlets have made these products widely available in France and beyond, it is a sign of hope for humanity.

Biodynamic farming goes even further: it views the soil as a self-contained living organism to be treated with respect and concentrates on bringing it back to health at a profound level. Biodynamics also introduces a spiritual dimension between the land and those who work on it, bringing an awareness to their work, how they relate to their environment and the impact on everything around them. The use of silicon-based products and plant concoctions such as yarrow, oak, dandelion or nettles, crushed up at different stages of their growth and turned into tinctures, aligns farming with the wider forces that are all around us. Biodynamics is a philosophy, or as the Greeks said, a *sophia* or wisdom, that gives a spiritual force to human action, binding us together with nature.

The phases of the moon provide the key to every action through the winemaking year, from harvest to vinification to aging to bottling. There are five different types of days that fall through the month: fruit days, flower days, root days, leaf days and lunar nodes, where the moon crosses the path of the sun.

Racking or bottling should be done only on fruit or flower days to ensure the wine is open and will develop its full fruity bouquet. Even the simplest observation reveals how different wines can taste after bottling. It is astonishing and instructive to see just what a difference, sometimes subtle but often extreme, that a few days makes in the taste and balance of your wine.

Biodynamic wines are part of the living world, and vibrantly reveal the taste of their *terroir* and the talent of their winemaker.

Steiner harnessed and channeled the knowledge of the ancient world, observed by generations of farmers, and gave it a new life through his teachings. In his third conference, he explained the actions and interactions of azote (nitrogen), sulphur, carbon, hydrogen and oxygen, and the importance of the spirit in nature. He also revealed the influence of the planet and the stars, the different effects of active and inactive nitrogen, and their influence on both plants and man. Sun and water interact strongly with calcium carbonate, silicon and the planets, and most powerfully with the moon. A storm that comes before a full moon is a moment of great strength in the growth of a plant and can be used, for example, to harness development after planting seeds.

The unarguable results of biodynamics, and the complexity of its interactions, forces us to question our actions and to become aware of a force higher than ourselves, which connects us to the world of minerals, plants and animals and makes us accountable, so as to help us organise our life as part of a community.

The biodynamic culture also helps us to develop our own human consciousness through a deepened respect for the wisdom of nature. It is a new paradigm that takes us forward to an era where fear, stress and anxiety give way to love, peace and harmony on our planet.

12

The Cross of the Visigoths

The Visigoth kingdom ruled between the 3rd and 8th century AD across what is now southern and southwest France. A tribe of Germanic origin that became powerful across Europe, Visigoth was long believed to mean "Goths of the West" in contrast to the Ostrogoths of the East, but today we know that Visigoths means "the wise goths" and the Ostrogoths were the "brilliant Goths".

Their long history of migration began with leaving their homeland in the Black Sea region, first to Dacia (today's Romania and Moldova) then onwards, from 376, to conquer Western Europe and settle large areas of the Holy Roman Empire in Hispania (Spain) and Aquitaine (France).

In total, their rule over these lands lasted for 250 years. The capital of the Visigoth kingdom was Toulouse until 507, when they were defeated by the Franks' King Clovis I at the battle of Vouillé. This defeat left them with a far smaller empire based around Septimanie (today's Languedoc, stretching over to Elne in Roussillon) and Provence. Here, they remained influential for a further 200 years, until the end of the 7th century, as well as in Spain, where their capital was Toledo. In 711, the Iberian kingdom was conquered by Muslim invaders from Africa, but pockets of Visigoth cultural and legal influence continued for many decades.

The religious beliefs of the Visigoth tribes centred around Arianism, the theological teachings of Arius from Alexandria in Egypt, who believed that Jesus Christ was a distinct figure separate from God and created directly by him. This belief was considered heretical by the Trinitarian doctrine followed by the Roman Catholic Church, and the Visigoths eventually converted to traditional Catholicism in 589.

The square cross that became part of the heraldry of the Visigoths seems to have been sculpted in marble by local Narbonne craftsmen in the first half of the 5th century, under the reign of Alaric II. It became the symbol of Septimanie and would later be known as the Languedoc Cross. Complex in its construction, it is studded with precious stones and carries the sign of alpha and omega suspended by two outstretched arms, representing the first and last letters of the Greek alphabet, signifying the beginning and end of time.

The marble block, which can be visited in the Musée Lapidaire in Narbonne, depicts a man holding one side of the cross in his left hand, the other in his right. At his feet, the sculptor has carved an animal, not the dog that you might expect at the feet of his master, but a crocodile. He is not chained up and seems to be a pet of the man, who may be an Egyptian monk. A pair of doves–universal symbols of sharing, communion and peace–drink together from a cup at the top of the cross.

My friend Professor Jacques Michaud pointed out the parallels between the values of this cross and those of my company, and today it stands as our emblem, an integral part of our logo, depicted on all official documents and on most of our labels.

The symbol of the cross is most likely one of the oldest images of mankind, perhaps as old as humanity itself. At its origin, a cross is the pictorial representation of primitive man standing upright and later of a man standing at a crossroads. The Egyptians used the Ankh Cross–the Cross of Life–to represent immortality and death and later, if we jump four centuries, it became the central image of the crucifixion of Jesus Christ by the Romans. It remains the symbol of Christ and Christianity.

Our cross is a little different from the Roman cross because all four of its branches are of equal length. Its origins lie in the East, in what is known as the Byzantine Empire, which became Visigoth after the invasion of Rome by the barbars.

The branches can be seen to represent the four directions of north, south, east and west; the four elements of air, fire, water and earth; the four seasons of spring, summer, autumn and winter; or simply the number four, which in tarot cards relates to stability and consistency (the Emperor); or the earth (Malkuth) in Kabbalah. Here, it serves to anchor man, to show him the manifestation of God on earth, to root him in a precise point in space and time. A little like the vine, rooted in its terroir, in its environment. Beyond this, 4 multiplied by the 3 points of the Trinity (represented by the two doves and the cup) gives the 12 months of the year; the 12 hours of the sun's summer solstice; the 12 steps to wisdom; and the 12 signs of the zodiac.

Reading the four branches as two intersecting bars gives a different significance. The vertical bar represents history - of the earth but also that revealed through the taste of an old wine–and lineage, the importance of roots and our ancestors. Its vertical position is also a reminder of the link between God and man, heaven and earth. It speaks to us of spirituality, again something that is always present in great wines. The horizontal bar represents the earth, but also fraternity–the group, the scrum.

The two bars also have particular significance in wine tasting, as it is possible to do a vertical, meaning several vintages of the same estate, perhaps from 2000 to 2005, or a horizontal, meaning the same vintage but several different estates, so perhaps the wines of La Clape in 2010.

The Narbonne cross is different again from the Occitan cross, which has 12 dots evenly spaced around its four axes, with no other decoration. What marks this cross out from all others is its relation to the vine, considered both a product of the earth and a link to the divine. Doves were the messengers of God on Noah's ark. They also represent the Virgin conception of the Annunciation, and the form taken by the Holy Spirit during the baptism of Jesus by John. Doves are the symbol of purity, peace and sharing, because they mate for life and work together to build their nest and raise their young, just as here they are drinking from the same cup. The cup also has a double significance; first that of transmutation, the Holy Grail and the search for the spirit. Beyond that, the cup contains wine and represents the mystery of fermentation, the door to God according to the 11th-century Persian poet Omar Khayyam. A cup was passed from guest to guest as a symbol of trust and conviviality during the great banquets of the Middle Ages, and the perhaps less raucous banquets of the 17th century...

The city of Narbonne itself has been linked to wine for countless generations; it was, after all, at the very centre of the first wine-producing region in the world.

13

Clos d'Ora

The realisation of a dream

Everything began with the vision I had while walking in this place in 1997.

I felt perfectly at one with nature, filled with a sense of love and wonder at the majesty of creation. That feeling in turn provoked a simple question: what was it about this place, these old stones, that allowed nature to reign supreme?

We were in La Livinière, against the foothills of the Montagne Noire, at an altitude of 250 metres, surrounded on all sides by *garrigue* and Mediterranean landscape. The remoteness of the spot, the jumble of marl and limestone, the sense of the earth rising and falling on all sides, called out to me, and I was deeply moved by a feeling of plenitude, of the abundance of nature.

The wine we produce here today was born from this feeling, and from the slow maturing of my spirit. It stands witness to my profound belief in a better future and my holistic interest in aligning positive thinking to spiritual power.

Its launch was a form of closure, the crowning of a cycle of 26 years of research, of meetings, of messages. It has opened the door to a new era where we can try humbly but actively to contribute to a movement toward achieving serenity, quietude, spirituality and prosperity.

Ora is the imperative form of the Latin verb *oro; orare* meaning "to beseech" or, more specifically "to pray": *ora pro nobis*, pray for us. In Greek, it means hour, or the idea of future growth. Our ancestors called this the principle of alpha and omega, both the beginning and the end of time, just as is found on the Visigoth cross. This is the moment known as ora (ΩPA).

The Trinity, represented by the past, present and future, allows man to be born, to grow, and to be raised in spirituality. And the end of time, as designated by the term apocalypse (revelation), does not signify the end of the world but a passing over to another time.

Today we are living in turbulent, agitated times, which seem to be hurtling us forward. And yet this is also a fascinating never-to-be-repeated era. Man has become more and more intelligent and yet less and less intuitive; he is surrounded by an ever-greater number of influences to the detriment of wisdom and sensitivity. Technology and modern communications often make us forget the truth of things, the reason that we are here. We live all too often gripped by fear and a general anxiety, scared of the future, and we can forget how to rely on our own abilities, our energy, spirit and subconscious.

To get past this, we need to confront one of the most difficult questions of our time; how to let go of the comfortable and the known to take a leap into the unknown. It is a challenge that stirs fear, tension, even violence. The dominant reaction can be to hold on tight to what we know, rather than open our hearts and minds to a new experience.

The time has come for us to connect once again to the universe, to realise our potential, be open to new experiences and be guided by our intuitions. In December 2004, after the Southeast Asian tsunami, it was noted that birds and animals cleared the zone before the great wave came. The phenomenon has been noted many times, leading to the expression "rats leaving a sinking ship". Living creatures have a great capacity for observation and intuition, and a connection to the higher orders of nature that allows them to sense danger instinctively, but we have become less and less adept at listening to this instinct.

Even if only a few people practice the power of positive thought and create a future based on peace, love and harmony, the impact will be powerful. It is a message that is both a biblical story and a universal truth; love thy neighbour, and do unto others as you would have them do unto you.

Not long after my revelation in this magical place, I had a feeling of lightness, of grace, of being soothed, and at the same time felt a need to connect myself with the essence of creation through meditation.

Meditation has become a regular practice for me, part of my daily life each morning. First to give thanks for the day ahead, and second to ensure that I am open to the possibilities of what lies ahead.

Meditation has changed my entire approach to life, allowing me to considerably reduce stress and anxiety and move beyond the physical. Simply watching the morning sunrise outside the window is enough to comprehend the perfect beauty of creation. This reinforces my convictions and makes sense of my world, allows me to cope better with any challenges and gives me the courage to rise above pessimism. Exploring new horizons and heading out toward the unknown gives life flavor and meaning. Despite this, it is clear that many of us have lost our sense of intuition, and are distracted by the countless possibilities of modern life, attracted by superficial things where one piece of new information is immediately replaced by the next in our consumer-driven society.

The farming world, traditionally, is founded on common sense and careful observation, on getting to know the local environment on an intimate level. But even today we have seen a creeping standardization, a blanket treatments of crops. Chemically synthetised products have replaced traditional cures, and we have been told that this standardization has supposedly increased the quality of all agricultural products, including wines. Viticulture has turned to the science of oenology and the promotion of standard winemaking techniques.

It is an evolution–even revolution–that has gone hand in hand with the growth of the market economy and the rise in popularity of varietal wines. At the same time we have seen a movement from wines that were essentially mysterious–made from a blend of several different varieties–to ones made to a recipe, lacking emotion. From the 1980s, varietal wines began to replace table wines, bringing with them a sense of bland reassurance for the consumer.

Are all these scientific advances useful? Certainly not when it comes to the vine. This is a plant that has been cultivated in France for over 24 centuries, a secular tradition that has accompanied us through successive civilisations. Wine, in its spiritual dimension, touches the face of God. It has been a symbol of friendship, exchange, celebration and ritual since Dionysos. That symbolic dimension is critical to retain.

The harm that has been done by the standardization of taste, the impact of chemicals on the food chain and on the quality of the water that we drink should wake us all up to the dangers of modern farming methods, and incite us to leave a better world and healthier planet for our children.

Much of the progress that we have made over the last century has been both useful and necessary, leading to significant advances. It has also led to an emerging middle class that is more urban and sedentary, requiring in turn new infrastructures and processed foods.

The principle advance in winemaking has been the ability to conserve wine for longer in bottle, protected from spoilage by the controlled use of sulphur. Because of this, wine is now able to travel, allowing the heritage and diversity of wine regions to be understood better around the world. The ability for a wine to age and improve in bottle is one of the indications of greatness. And yet for this to have meaning in the future we must, as Rudolf Steiner points out, take care of the fertility of our soils and have a respect for our immediate environment and for our wider countryside.

We do not have to accept that intensive farming must replace our traditional knowledge. That would be a regression. A farmer–*paysan* in French–must take care of the land–*le paysage* in French. His estate is a living thing, part of the land, and should be treated with respect. To maintain the links to the land, a farmer needs to concentrate on his crops and a winemaker on his vines. But even that is not enough. We need to remember that biodiversity guarantees the balance, sometimes subtle, of the entire ecosystem. It is as essential to take care of the insects, wildlife and microbial life of the soils as it is the vines. That is the only way to guarantee the fertility and balance of plants for the long-term, as well as the quality of the fruit that they produce. It does not take a university degree to see this, just the common sense to observe what is happening around us, and the strength to resist taking the easy route.

Agriculture should nourish the planet, but the pressure to produce endless amounts of food is stretching it to breaking point. We need to find a way to break the status quo, to find alternatives such as organic or non-genetically modified farming styles and encourage consumers to eat according to the seasons. We need also to learn to eat less meat and to increase our consumption of water and cereals.

Wine is no longer an essential part of our daily nutritional intake. Over the past 30 years it has become instead a drink that we enjoy for pleasure. In wine-producing countries, the levels of consumption keep dropping, even while climbing elsewhere. Over the next decade, we will see vineyards planted in nearly every country in the world–a great chance for humanity because wine, consumed with moderation, can awaken the conscience, create social links, cement community life and even lead to a spiritual awakening.

We need to stop running toward that which is technically correct in favour of that which tastes good and is authentic and respects natural differences. There are 6,000 grape varieties in the world, and most consumers concentrate on the 10 most well-known. We have a way to go. The vine has the capacity to amaze and delight if we respect this simple formula: soil, vineyard plot, grape variety. We will gain nothing by endlessly replanting chardonnay and cabernet sauvignon–to simply mention the best known–instead of respecting the abundance of local grape varieties that can reveal an intrinsic sense of place, as well as building a long-term future based on a wine region's identity and culture. Consumers and producers could in this way move away from the destruction of globalisation and build for the long-term.

I want to argue also for a greater sensitivity toward our soils and subsoils, our biotopes and our precious landscapes. Viticulture should be a standard-bearer for how to treat this planet. Its potential for growth across numerous complex markets and the increasing demand for quality from consumers represents a fantastic opportunity for our industry that it must seize. The technical developments over the last 30 years have been undeniably profitable for the wine industry. But it must now reinvent itself to safeguard its own future and to honour its roots.

I would go so far as to compare the current move toward drinking less but better and with greater awareness to recent advances in physics, specifically with the discovery of the Higgs boson particle that has so enthused the scientific community. Both have opened new perspectives and revealed new possibilities. Both Steiner for biodynamics and Max Planck for quantum mechanics worked at the start of the 20th century and changed received ideas at a fundamental level. One hundred years later, these visionary geniuses continue to open the minds of those who follow them. I am fascinated by the power of their beliefs and the strength they showed in following their ideas wherever they led them. Steiner was able to resist the many agricultural "advances" that were going on all around him, such as using potash as a fertiliser, and instead advocate a radically different approach. Planck revolutionized our understanding of atomic and subatomic processes in the way that Ludwig Boltzmann revolutionized our understanding of atoms and the physical properties of matter. All were deserving of the greatest respect and revealed so much to me as I studied their ideas, leading me to a greater understanding of quantum theory. Steiner's key intention with his 1929 book was to wake farmers up to the importance of a holistic approach. In nine conferences, he laid out the fundamentals of his approach, as well as the practical daily ways to put his ideas into action.

Drawing on these lessons, it seems clear to me that the driving force of all our actions should be an intention to do good. At Clos d'Ora, we wanted to create a place where the dominant feeling is of peace, love and harmony. To do this we adapted not only our farming methods, but also our very way of being and living, and our faith in ourselves.

The ruins of the old sheep farm that was located on the land was rebuilt stone by stone by my friend Jean-Luc Piquemal, with the wise advice of architect Jean-Frédéric Luscher. Above the barrel cellar and winery, seamlessly integrated into the whole, we constructed a welcoming space dedicated to meditation and quiet contemplation.

In the vineyards we introduced traditional methods of farming using animals instead of machinery for labour. Horses and mules are part of the natural balance, the interconnection between minerals, plants, animals and humans. The horse is a symbolic animal that here carries out the precise work of opening up the soil during ploughing. Its hooves do not compact the soils as a tractor would, and they protect the microbial health and aeration of the soils, as well as allowing the force of the stars and the heavens to penetrate the soils and subsoils below. The plant receives not only the message but also the feeling of love. It is paradoxical–both highly complex and extremely simple. And of course avoiding tractors means our carbon footprint is considerably reduced. The wine that results from this approach has its own highly distinct personality, one that reveals the influence of its astonishing *terroir*, where vines are grown at altitude on mainly clay soils for the carignan and mourvèdre, largely marl for the grenache and limestone for the syrah.

These ancient cultivation methods connect the earth to the universe, and we have been able to produce a heavenly nectar from this exceptional place, one that flows from the use of biodynamics and from unlocking the power of quantum farming with our dedicated team.

Each bottle of Clos d'Ora, wherever it travels and whenever it is opened, carries within it the flavor of love that flows naturally through its vines.

14

Quantum wine

Full awareness

I recently studied the fundamentals of quantum mechanics as discovered and explained by Max Planck and was fascinated to see how they can translate to personal development. The writings of Étienne Klein, Sven Ortoli, Stephen Hawking and Vadim Zeland helped me to uncover the principles and their application to our daily lives. I am not a physicist and am not looking to become one, but am instead interested in how these theories can help me to evolve within my own profession and give me a sense of purpose.

The thought experiment of Schrödinger's cat and the influence of the observer on events, the binary opposition of things and beings, all open our consciousness to new horizons, new ways of being and thinking. By meditating on the world of atoms, electromagnetic waves and photons, you enter into an intangible, vibratory space and move closer to an understanding of the relationship between microcosm and macrocosm, between our interior and exterior world.

All matter is energy. Quantum physics, at its heart, teaches us that everything in our universe is energy, vibrating at one speed or another, and that this ocean of energy connects us all. In the human body, each organ possesses its own particular frequency. Man is also composed of between 75 percent and 80 percent water, and yet Jacques Benveniste's work on water memory–the belief that water retains a memory of substances previously dissolved within it as an explanation of the mechanism by which homeopathic remedies work–was for a long time contradicted and dismissed. Recently the virologist, AIDS specialist and Nobel Prize–winning professor Luc Montagnier took up some of the methodology of Benveniste, lending credence to the earlier research and suggesting his fellow scientist was a "modern Galileo". Montagnier found indications in numerous experiments that water retained a memory of molecules. Wine is also 85 percent water–surely it, too, can have a memory. Wine, as we have said, is a multifaceted drink. My intention here is not to scientifically prove the theory of water memory but simply to affirm that wine carries with it information relating to its grape variety, the place where it is grown and the soil that has nurtured it. The vibrations of the winemaker, his spirit and state of mind also have a physical impact on the fledgling wine from the moment of harvest until the moment of bottling.

My personal approach comprises feeling, thinking, and conceptualising the final wine before harvesting a single grape and then, at the moment of harvest, allowing my intuition to guide me toward the right decisions. For this, I need to feel connected and in harmony with nature, to be at one with the living world both physically and spiritually. By tasting the berries throughout the month of September, I begin to understand both their state of readiness for harvest and the quality potential of that year's wine. This exercise is the best way to decide on the right moment for picking and is something that I like to share with my team. Analysis of the grapes in the laboratory is simply used to back up the decisions that we have already taken. Billions of yeast cells will transform the sugar into alcohol during fermentation. These too are living beings, and their action will establish the characteristics of each grape variety.

The singular nature of wine, its potential for aging, its connection with the soils and subsoils all heightened my desire to search out a new way that would respect the precepts of Rudolf Steiner while going beyond the practices of biodynamic farming. I wanted to go further by harnessing the power of the mind and our connection to the universe. I wanted to create a wine able to resonate with spirit and soul.

This is the fourth level, the message, that allows us to search out the best of a place and give it both an awareness and a vibratory field. In this way the "teacher" can feel the soul of a wine. Being able to open yourself up to this ability requires extensive tasting experience together with a deep understanding of your surroundings and a spiritual awakening.

The farmer is traditionally a person with a clairvoyant perception of nature, able to make sense of wisdom received over many years of practical experience, someone with a profound understanding that feelings and beliefs should take precedence over intellect. Someone who works regularly with the land is often subconsciously capable of connecting his spirit to his soul, his conscious to his unconscious, and is able to get the best out of soils, plants, animals and lands, often purely through intuition. He is able to unlock an interior understanding, an energy that passes not through words but through physical gestures. Living in the open air inevitably means he is in greater contact with the forces of the universe, part of the cycle of the stars, and he is able to follow their influence, notably that of the moon, and to let his year be guided by the seasons and the climate.

Steiner was clear about the influence of nitrogen in the air on our imagination and thought processes. He asked that we visualize the nitrogen process, following its path from the atmosphere to the soil and plant and back again into the air. Steiner saw nitrogen as a connection between the farmer and the elements of earth, air, water and fire, and the quantum approach seems to me to be highly complementary to those beliefs.

Deep thinking and meditation brings an undeniable harmony

to daily life, suppressing the fear that is often rooted in our ego. Profound joy and happiness are the rewards awaiting those who raise their consciousness, try to understand the universe, and live in the belief of a higher being and the presence of a divine order.

I believe that we must learn to leave our ego behind if we are to be open to a spiritual life. The history of our civilization teaches us that there have been examples of men who have lived among us, incarnations of this divinity on earth–Moses, Buddha, Socrates, Jesus, Mohammed–who carried a message of wisdom and transcendence. In our own modest way, through meditation we can attempt to understand the teachings of these masters and feel the cosmic pulse of the universe.

Many of us wish to search for happiness and joy, but our experience has made us distrustful of the possibility. Mankind often suffers from neuroses and depressions, often induced by our own self-limiting need to find security by following the pack, scared of what could happen if we search for our own truth. We behave like sheep and live by proxy without ever finding our own way or looking for what makes us truly ourselves.

It is often easier to blame others for our problems rather than commit to living our own lives, full of surprises, discoveries, creativity. We need to wake up and have courage if we are to take responsibility for ourselves. Freedom and true change come from a break with the tired beliefs that have bound us in the past, the false security offered by conforming to other people's ideals.

The first step comes with getting to know ourselves, lifting the cover off our own profound nature, freeing our spirits. It means distinguishing between our fears and our deepest beliefs, distinguishing between actions that are driven by our thoughts and the ones that are driven by our souls. Our consciousness creates both fears and joys, while our unconscious feels love and hate, and the deepest emotions that guide us. Only our soul can connect us to the higher universe, where information can be divined through intuition and premonition.

We consciously chose to create in Clos d'Ora a wine inspired by quantum theories; true to its own nature, open to the universe, born of its own *terroir*, carrying a textured message of peace, love and harmony.

I needed to check the merits of our approach to this wine. Thanks to my friend Jean Louis Gavard, I met up with Georges Vieilledent, who is a specialist in energy and informational fields, using cutting-edge techniques (see pages XVII-XXIV: quantum wine). The first images that he produced were fascinating. They revealed the expression of the wine, both superb and moving, expressing the intentions that guided me at the moment of the creation of the Clos d'Ora project. The first expression coming from these photos was the manifestation of the life, beautiful, with an energy force emanating from the photos that was both beautiful and piercing. The composition of the structure, richer and more precise for Clos d'Ora, showed sun-like rays emanating from the wine, a universal logic belonging to living things in full expression. The influence of Clos d'Ora gives all sense to the work and the attention, physical, emotional and spiritual, that we have devoted in both the vineyards and cellars during the making of this wine. The universality of the message is striking, as is the power, which seems both simple and incontrovertible–beauty, delicacy, light and transcendence together with feelings, profound and touching the sacred.

The soul of this *terroir* inspired me to blend only grapes that are most profoundly rooted in the South of France–grenache, syrah, mourvèdre and carignan, farmed biodynamically–and from them to begin to realise a dream. Over time, the intention is to create unshakeable links between taste and beauty, the *terroir* and its message, and to understand how all of this fits in to the universal matrix. It is impossible to be anything but humbled and awed by the realisation that all matter is both unimaginably large and indescribably tiny, from the building blocks of the atom and the Higgs boson (also known as the God particle), to the farthest reaches of the cosmos and the Big Bang at the heart of the creation of our universe. Uncovering the nature of humanity lies in this search.

Wine can help man answer his most basic needs–to eat, to drink, to breath and to move–while also drawing him toward a richer and more complex life. Wine is a form of transmutation, because it carries within it the aromas of fruits, the taste of *terroir*, the soul of a place and the perfection of creation. This is a fact that has been recognised and celebrated since Dionysos.

Quantum wine respects a process of rigorous vinification and aging, of mastering the art of blending and of farming biodynamically; of delivering waves of emotion, vibrations, resonances and with them a message of peace. Love guides us because it is the source of our creative power and it embodies the perfection of the universe. We are mindful of every single step in the process of creating this wine, from pruning the vine to the final bottling, and each moment along the way from harvest, aging and blending. And with each step we are carried along by the harmonious vibrations felt on this spot of earth, guiding us forward.

It has taken courage and hard work to define our objectives and beliefs, born of a dream that became a desire and then an objective. It has taken 15 years to reveal the potential of these stones, this soil, this land that is perfect for meditation but also for the advent of wine.

Biodynamic farming, when linked to quantum beliefs, has been essential in creating a wine that is in total harmony with nature. Our winery is connected to the universe by having its vats out in the open air, allowing an exchange between the forces of the cosmos and those of the planet, ensuring steady and successful fermentation. Barrel aging in the darkened quiet of the cellars gives a sense of well-being deepened by an exchange and a vibration between the wine, oak and air, all contributing to a slow softening of the tannins.

Blending is a fundamental step in the realisation of the work. Our vinification techniques are as natural as possible, respecting the essential nature of the grapes and the year that has shaped them, but blending is the moment that will establish the potential of the wine. The choice of harvest date, depending on the ripeness of the bunches, allows us to extract the essence of the grapes, ensuring healthy berries where the tannins can be gently extracted to provide structure and impart a long life. This takes a scientific understanding of the effects of the year's climatology, a precise analysis of the different levels of acidity, pH and tannins within the grape but also the intuition to understand the perfect moment for intervention. It is the art of precision viticulture.

Once samples of each variety–which have been kept separate during the process of transforming the sugar into alcohol–from each of the eight vineyard plots have arrived in the tasting room, a long process begins. Time slows down at this point, and the vibrations in the room seem to rise or fall depending on the sensations of the different samples and our interactions with each one. The creation of a wine is an adventure every time, and it requires a sense of aestheticism, a complicity and a harmony between each member of the team, all working towards the same goal–to create a masterpiece.

There is art in wine. God created us in his image and gave us free will, but also the ability to think and to strive toward the creation of something larger and more precious than ourselves. Happiness, joy, love and creation are not reserved for the select few but are available to us all. In this first tasting session with eight wines, held in monastic silence, the first task is to acknowledge the importance of the moment.

The next step is to rank the quality of each, grape variety by grape variety, and to understand how they may complement and build upon each other. Each one of us will try, over the next few hours, to create our own best possible blend without recourse to the reality of the volumes of wine aging in the cellars. This will result in three blends–one from the cellar master, one from the technical director and one from me. They will be poured into three glasses and all will be tasted blind, with no indication of whose blend is which. The first comments simply allow us to assess the work we have done and the quality of the blends and their component parts. After a second tasting, accompanied by detailed notes, we reveal what is contained in each blend, so as to allow a better understanding of where the blends approach each other and where they diverge. This is laborious, meticulous work, where every single element must be taken into account–the taste and feeling of a wine can be altered by just the tiniest fraction more or less of any single element. We are guided by the desire for excellence, and we focus on listening to both our internal and external consciousness, to be led by our physical senses and our intuition in the search for the essential truth of each wine, and the truth of the *terroir* that it comes from.

The first vintage is always the most difficult, because to create the best possible wine means understanding the heart of its personality, and that is something that only reveals itself slowly, vintage by vintage over the course of many years. This first time, we chose the final blend after three or four hours of tasting. The final choice is always unanimous. We then retaste the blend with food, to be certain that the wine is both amplified and enhanced by the flavours that it is paired alongside. Red wine is not made to be drunk young, but rather over the course of five, 10, 20 years or longer, and it is fundamental that it can be drunk with food. It is rare to hit perfection with the first blending session, and the entire thing may be redone two, three even four times to refine the proportions of the blend, and to take into account the effects of the lunar calendar and the influence that the planets will have on each grape variety.

When we have defined the backbone of the wine, its expression and its character, we have to adjust the final volume of each component. Transforming a theoretical blend into a final wine is itself a form of revelation, the result of both careful methodology and a form of divine inspiration. The wine will spend at least 12 months in French oak that has come from the highest quality, fully sustainable forests where trees are replanted as they are felled.

After oak aging, each barrel is tasted individually and this magic process should reveal a complex interaction between the tannins in the wine and the tannins in the oak. Each barrel has its own personality, with subtle differences from its neighbour. If we have done our job well, the result will be more than the sum of its parts with greater complexity and elegance than was revealed when tasted in isolation. After the final blend, the wine needs to spend at least another few weeks in a large vat to settle down and reach the optimal atmospheric conditions for bottling, something that must only take place on fruit days within the lunar calendar. We sometimes refine the wine with a little organic egg white to refine its texture, but the decision is taken each year, depending on the vintage. There are no hard-and-fast rules here, we respond to what the wine tells us. Finally, it spends a few months resting in bottle before beginning its journey to our clients.

Each vintage will have a different aging potential, certainly, but Clos d'Ora is a wine made to deepen and evolve over time. The blend is a result of the infinite ability of these grape varieties, on this *terroir*, to carry a message of harmony and enlightenment through their flavour. It is the result of a long voyage of discovery, conceived, imagined and realised by the grace of God.

15

The Song of Songs

For a better world

The Old Testament's Song of Solomon, or Song of Songs, is at its heart an ode to love. It gives us evidence of the physical, sensual connection between man and woman. It is the text that symbolises, in my mind, human transcendence, the visceral need for love in all its forms–in the flesh but also spiritual love, together with a love for nature and for the fruit of the vine. All of these forms of love are essential in reaching a greater understanding of ourselves and so allowing us to build a close relationship with one another. We can even draw an analogy here between the act of kissing and the act of drinking wine.

Wine, in this sense, is a sacred drink. The grape has transmuted into something divine. Its creation is perfect and reveals how God is everywhere, beyond individual beliefs or religions. The universe is infinite and we try our best, thanks to the discoveries and continued searching of our physicists and scientists, to get a better understanding of what lies within and outside of ourselves. These are fascinating voyages. The research of men such as Leonardo da Vinci, Copernicus, Galileo, Freud, Einstein and Planck has allowed us to uncover essential truths about evolution and human behavior.

Planck, through his discovery of quantum mechanics, brought us a greater understanding of the infinity of the universe and every particle contained within it. Sven Ortoli and Jean-Pierre Pharabod, in their book *The Song of Quantum*, began to edit questions about our role in the universe. "The fundamental nature of time is that it passes, that is what distinguishes it from space", wrote physicist and philosopher of science Etienne Klein. "The future inexorably becomes the present and then the past. It is this succession of events that we call time".

I have always believed that by creating a wine in perfect balance between *terroir* and grape, I am contributing to a different definition of time. A definition that takes into account the character of the vintage and how it pours its own sense of time and place into the wine–offering the merest hint today of what it will become tomorrow.

Together we are contributing to the birth of a new world, one that is born both of new discoveries and the advent of the internet. Time has speeded up exponentially, and we are bombarded with information on all sides. All our secular beliefs are being tested. Physicists tell us today that the universe has been constantly expanding ever since the Big Bang–an idea that is both fascinating and terrifying, because it brings up questions that we don't have the answers to. But all of this expansion of knowledge is also an opportunity to write a new chapter for humanity.

Some believe that we are at the end of one cycle and the beginning of another, but even among the confusion and flux, we must be careful to pass on certain essential truths to our children and to future generations. As human beings, we must hold on to our link with the divine, our knowledge of our own trinity–body, soul and spirit.

I would like, in some small way, to set out the links between the sacred texts of the Bible and the quantum world, because it seems to me that wine can be a conductor that carries with it an emotional charge able to unite mankind. Clearly wine is not intended to meet the nutritional needs that man has for nourishment in the way that wheat, rice and water do, base elements essential for our survival. Wine instead nourishes a different part of man. Consumed moderately, carefully and thoughtfully, it can stimulate our sense of generosity and tolerance, essential qualities for living in a community. In both the Jewish and Christian tradition, it has transcended the generations, accompanied the search for truth.

All of my great wines have been created in this spirit; in the hope that they will contribute toward a more harmonious world, with less fear and a greater receptivity to universal love for ourselves and our families, to help us be open to the infinite possibilities of the universe.

Some will inevitably find this ideal utopian, even extravagant. But I have always believed in becoming free, able to live each day with the minimum of restraint and the maximum of happiness. It is a never-ending spiritual journey, but I am on the path, putting one step in front of another. I feel a ray of hope in this ever-changing world and believe there are opportunities being created today as never before. We must remain positive and open to a better future. If each of us joins together in peace, love and harmony, we can find a new way to live. Generosity and happiness will be our new goals.

II

THE ESTATES

16

Domaine de Villemajou

Passing the torch

Whether it is the passing on of knowledge or skills, the act of handing down an inheritance to the next generation is one of the most beautiful gifts that a parent can give to a child, alongside their time, patience and love. The rest is superfluous.

"You are so lucky to be doing your first harvest at 10 years old", my father said to me. "Do you understand why? I had to wait until I was 25 to make my first wine". No, I did not understand at the time. All I knew was that it meant I had to work. And work hard. From 5 in the morning until 1 in the afternoon throughout the two months of summer across all 60 hectares of my family estate. It was tough, without a doubt, but today the memories flood back as if it was yesterday.

I remember the happiness and freedom of being out in the vines with my sister Guylaine. We watched the sun coming up, ran for miles each day and worked together, pitching in all together as one big family. Alongside us was my father–the leader, clearly–while my mother was in charge of the troops. She was the *mousseigne* – chief picker in the local Languedoc dialect, the one who worked the quickest and who set the pace for the harvest.

Each evening, the family would gather at my grandmother Paule's house. Her husband, who left her 2.5 hectares of vines, had died in 1948 and she–a tiny woman, weighing perhaps 40 kilos at most–had brought up their nine children alone armed with little more than love and a boundless work ethic. A true matriarch, born on January 1, 1900, she passed through the century with valour, courage and warmth and was the foundation of our family. Her children (seven still lived in the village around her at the time), their wives and 14 grandchildren formed a happy, noisy tribe. A few years later, when she was no longer with us, I honoured her in the way I knew best–with a wine–Domaine-Sainte-Paule.

I have always been grateful to my father for sending me into the cellars during harvest. Three weeks at the Cave de Villemajou to vinify the new vintage, with no regard for either the school term or the rugby schedule. Twice a week I would train with him outside as the night fell. We ran around the streets and pathways of Corbières, guided by the light of the moon. Often, after a day's work, I would run back home. Saturdays I left the cellars just after lunch to go play with my team in Narbonne. At the final whistle, I would hitch-hike back home to Villemajou to do my chores. I was in charge of the grape press and was taught the different ways of operating it, depending on the type of grape. The equipment was pretty basic and the pressing cycles were all set manually, giving me the impression that I was playing a crucial role in the process. I took everything terribly seriously and was bursting with pride that my father had entrusted me with this. Sometimes I needed to visit the cellars late at night, around 10pm, to operate the final few turns of the screw. By this point I was 16 years old and had begun to drive–without a license–along the small country roads of Corbières where I passed nobody but rabbits and wild boars.

I would get to the cellars to do my "round" as night was falling, heady with youth and a newfound sense of freedom, leaving the car window open so I could breathe the fresh air. It was my way of feeling alive. One night, when I was not paying attention, I ended up in a ditch. Somehow I managed to get the car back on the road, but then I made the fatal mistake of trying to get home with a tire that was so flat that I was limping along on the metal hub. By the time I got home, the car had caught fire. I panicked and called my uncle out to help me, but the damage had been done and the car was a write-off. My parents were out eating with friends, so I miserably headed off to bed. In the morning, my father said nothing about it–and never did. Maybe he felt a little guilty for having let me use his old Renault 4. Or more likely he knew that I had learnt my lesson and that nothing he said was going to make it either better or worse.

Every day that I could, when everyone stopped for lunch between 1 and 2pm, I headed out into the vines to check on the ripening of the grapes. I was obsessed by the torturous progression of the carignan and grenache. These particular varieties somehow taste different from the very first moment, and are deeply affected by their *terroir*. Their skins are usually firm, the pulp dense but soft and well balanced. Sometimes before heading home in the evening I would impulsively follow the little stream that ran through the estate and across country roads all the way to the village. I was always happiest when I met no cars along the way and was just alone with the rising moon. When clouds were out, the sky took on fantastical patterns. I would walk home briskly, imagining all sorts of menacing presences, which turned out of course to be simply the lengthening shadows.

The soils of Villemajou hold the memories of both my childhood and adolescence. I now fully understand the emotional attachment that a winemaker can feel toward his vineyard. Our vines are at the very heart of the Corbières appellation near the village of Boutenac, grown on remarkably homogenous soils of limestone boulders that were first formed five million years ago in the Miocene era. Warm red stones abound, holding the heat of the day and reflecting it back to the grapes each night. The surrounding countryside is soft and round; with rolling hills covered with pine forest. The estate is marked by its traditional old carignan vines that reach 80 years old and more, blended with the syrah and mourvèdre that my father planted to add complexity to his wine almost 40 years ago.

I suggested to several winemaking friends, around a decade ago, to submit a request to the French appellations body (INAO) for the recognition of the exceptional quality of the Boutenac area. After four years of interactions, an official enquiry was set up in 2005 to study the soils and assess the quality of the resulting wines. After long deliberations, the area was finally awarded the recognition of Boutenac Cru.

Villemajou is our yardstick, the barometer of our vines. It has its own distinct personality that arises from the combination of its soil, the dry heat of its climate and its Mediterranean grapes. The first-ever vintage to be bottled here was 1973. At the time its gold label was written off by buyers and wine experts, who told us to change the label to something more modern. Today, 40 years later, the same label has become iconic, recognisable at a single glance. Domaine de Villemajou is a symbol of reliable quality. I am proud to continue in the footsteps of my father, and I see this wine as a gift given to me by destiny. A bridge between the past, present and future.

17

Domaine de Cigalus

Live on the land and respect it

Respecting the land that we live on seems the very least that we can do. The quality of life itself depends on it, and I have spent the majority of my adult life trying to honour that truth.

The first time I saw Domaine de Cigalus was a Friday afternoon in April 1995. The estate agent had given me clear directions and I found myself, having turned off a small road, in front of a large house that had clearly been abandoned for some time. Off to the side were a few small buildings in the same perilous state, and beyond stretched vineyards–a few also looking a little tired–growing around a valley against the backdrop of mountains that I knew intimately. In the distance I could see the medieval château of Saint-Martin-de-Tocques, bought and renovated five years previously, standing 60 metres above. I was used to seeing it close-up, on the northeastern outskirts of Saint-André-de-Roquelongue, the village where I was born. The property that I was looking at would take me just five short kilometres away from this village that I knew and loved.

Walking in the vines, I felt totally at home. The climate here was a little dryer than in my village because we were getting further from the sea, and I remember a strong sensation of the warmth of the earth, battered by sun and wind, washing over me. We were also close to the Abbey of Fontfroide and the neighbouring Notre-

Dame-de-Gaussan, and the two served to awaken both my spiritual values and my love of history.

I wandered through the rooms of the house, headed into the cellar, then spent some time simply looking out at the landscape, enveloped by the calm that seemed to reign over the vineyard. I had fallen for the charm of these buildings, even in their unloved state. It had taken less than a minute to fall in love and not much more to imagine the family that I wanted to build here with my then-fiancée Ingrid. The following Monday, as soon as I was able, I became the owner of Domaine de Cigalus. It was truly the beginning of a metamorphosis–not just for this estate but for my life. After a year of renovations, my new wife and I were finally able to move in. In 1998, our daughter Emma joined us. Her brother Mathias arrived in 2000, and Cigalus became the cradle of our new family. At the same time, I became convinced that I wanted to create a wine that respected the strong energy that I felt in this place. This led me to biodynamics as a new way to cultivate the soil, to set aside any chemical fertilisers or weedkillers and to instead fully respect what nature had given me the land.

I had long been aware of the benefits of the tiny daily doses of homeopathic medicine that I took. It had truly transformed my life and strengthened my immune system. It also made me understand just how every one of us is an individual, just as each plot of land is different. I couldn't pinpoint exactly when these realisations about my own body were extended to my land, but I expect it was related to the birth of my children. Little by little I felt more deeply responsible for the world around me, and I knew that I wanted my children to grow up in a place that would nourish them. Perhaps it related back to my own idyllic childhood in the heart of a beautiful place. Or perhaps I simply became more and more disillusioned with the processed foods that were becoming ever more prevalent. I started to realise that something better and less expensive was possible if we took things back into our own hands. Homeopathy seemed to be in perfect alignment with my life and my philosophy.

There is a homeopathic medicine for the earth: it is called biodynamics. All I needed was to extend the philosophy of caring for my own health to my environment. Biodynamics means listening to the earth and giving it what it needs. Shortly after buying Domaine de Cigalus, I decided to keep the old vines of merlot, cabernet sauvignon, cabernet franc, caladoc, syrah, carignan, mourvèdre and grenache, and to extend the vineyard by planting grapes in new plots. I wanted to make an unusual white blend and so chose chardonnay, sauvignon and viognier. After three years, I was happy with the results. The new method of farming was succeeding more quickly than we had ever imagined, and we were producing exceptional wines. Biodynamics creates whites that are refreshing and balanced, full of floral aromatics both subtle and enveloping, with a wonderful burst of minerality. The reds develop complexity, elegance and a rich mouthfeel. The earth itself becomes more malleable and easier to work. Wildlife of all kinds have made this place their home, as well as at least seven different varieties of herbs, happily co-existing with the vines.

We have learnt to commune with the earth at Cigalus, and it nourishes us in return.

18

Château Laville-Bertrou

Learning to taste

Understanding how to taste wine is like learning to appreciate life itself. It is an art that helps you to become a better version of yourself. While walking in the vines, I feel connected to the *terroir* by touching the soil, running it through my fingers, smelling it. It is an excellent way to understand the saline quality of soils. Rocks overwhelm the landscape here–limestone, schist and clay–somehow heightened by the aridity of the climate that is softened only by the morning dew, or by the wind that blows damp if arriving from the sea, dry if from the interior. Then there are vines and myriad herbs and plants that push up through the soil: thyme, rosemary, broom, mulberry, cistaceae, pine, oak and bay trees, each transmitting something of their essence to the *terroir*. And beyond all this, there are the contours of the land itself; steep slopes planted for as long as anyone can remember. Gentle in some places, dizzyingly steep hillsides in others, all located to the south and east of the village, within earshot of the church bells that call out the rhythm of the day, drawing people together and dominating the life of the village.

The winemakers of La Livinière were grouped together in the 1990s by Maurice Piccinini and have since showed an exceptional ability to market their wines–something that I benefitted from when I arrived. I would also like to thank the Bertrou family, and particularly Nicole and Jean, who have become my friends. They first asked me for my winemaking advice in 1997 and allowed me to slowly but surely take on a bigger role in the running of the estate. Both concentrating on their careers elsewhere, they wanted simply to retain a symbolic part of the property in memory of their father, and it fills me with happiness to see that the family banner continues to fly above the estate, in honour of patriarch Paul Bertrou.

Finally there is the village, built in a circle unfurling around Château Laville-Bertrou like a shell encircling a snail. Its borders are protected by houses built in the dry stone typical of the Minervois, with narrow winding alleyways stretching upwards toward the limestone plateau and the Montagne Noire beyond. This mountain range is the southernmost extent of the Massif Central and stands watch over the village. The shadow of the mountain casts formidable shadows over the landscape, by turns majestic and severe, creating a specific microclimate with hot days but fresh nights that ensure the vine leaves don't suffer from the heat that would otherwise reign here.

Carignan, grenache, syrah and mourvèdre all benefit from this microclimate. Each one is harvested, sent into the cellars and vinified separately, just as precious stones have to be carefully selected before becoming glittering jewels. I learnt the truth of this viticultural approach by listening, dreaming and feeling the vibrations of this *terroir*. La Livinière is the kingdom of syrah, because the fresh nights deliver a fruity yet spicy punch. After sparingly blending with grenache and mourvèdre and–in hot years only–carignan, you are rewarded with wines that are both powerful and classical, with an innate sense of character. Walking on the plateau that sits above the village reminds me of this and continues to move me, every single time.

"Wine is nature dignified as a sacrament", wrote Paul Claudel, reflecting my feelings perfectly. The journey grapes take from the vineyard to the spirit is a long one, but we can glimpse the poetry of their voyage in the wines of Château Laville-Bertrou.

19

Château L'Hospitalet

Sharing an art de vivre

Sharing is everything. The more we can develop radiance in our own lives, the more we can use it to benefit those around us.

Jacques Ribourel, the celebrated property developer and owner of Château L'Hospitalet, was looking at me. We were sitting face to face on a glorious February morning in 2002, sizing each other up like two rugby players squaring off during a match, and I got the distinct impression that he was enjoying my look of surprise.

He had just asked me to buy L'Hospitalet, confiding that it was time for him to move on to other projects. "You are young, ambitious, and you understand this land, you belong here. You will know how to build on what I have created, to harness it and no doubt improve on it. And besides, winemaking is what you do. It is not what I do". Hearing this, it would be easy to think that I was about to become the owner of L'Hospitalet and that the deal was done. In reality nothing was further from the truth.

A few hours earlier, I had been enjoying a relaxed lunch with my family, with no idea that a man that I knew by reputation only was about to change everything with a simple telephone call. Standing 15 kilometres from Narbonne in the heart of a national park in Massif de la Clape, Château L'Hospitalet is comprised of an assortment of buildings, some dating back to the 16th century, surrounded by 1,000 hectares of *garrigue* and 60 hectares of vines. Behind the hill that dominates the vineyard is the Mediterranean Sea. It is an exceptional spot. Everyone in France has heard of L'Hospitalet–not least because of its purchase in 1991 by this man, who turned it into one of the most exceptional examples of wine tourism in the whole of the country.

The phone call came out of the blue, and a thousand questions were forming in my head as I climbed into my car and drove the beautiful winding route from Narbonne to L'Hospitalet. Pine trees, *garrigue*, vines and limestone outcrops accompanied my drive. I arrived at the fork in the road that leads down to the entrance. The path meandered through the vines, and I recognised the familiar shapes of syrah and mourvèdre. I parked and walked into the outlying courtyard where I saw an apiary, a shop selling regional delicacies and the entrance to a museum dedicated to local wildlife. I pushed open the gate to walk on farther and found myself in the main courtyard surrounded by buildings that contained an art gallery and a glassware boutique. To my right were two restaurants and in front a building that had just become a hotel a few years earlier. It was an incredible achievement, heightened by an atmosphere that was both playful and welcoming.

I had been here not long before, interested in exploring the possibilities of wine tourism. As surprising as it seems, 25 centuries earlier, this place was a Phoenician island between Narbonne and the Mediterranean. Not only that, but it was the true cradle of vines in France, because it was here that the first vineyards were cultivated. I idly wondered how the landscape must have looked at the time, with vines planted haphazardly, as there were no neat rows in French vineyards until the 17th century. L'Hospitalet was owned in the 13th century by the Hospices de Narbonne, then in the 15th century by the Hôpital de Saint-Just. Wine was always made here, even when it was a hospice, something that inspired its most recent incarnation as a place to promote healing and health. I was lost in these thoughts when a matronly woman approached and suggested that I join Mr. Ribourel in the restaurant.

I looked out over the courtyard from my table and was once again struck by what I saw; wine was clearly the central element–vines, winery, cellar, tasting room, a boutique, all nods to the sensory universe that surrounds wine. There was something for the taste, the eyes, the nose...nothing seemed to have been forgotten. Nothing? I realised that I had not heard any music. A shame.

This magical place seemed to breathe the *art de vivre* and the gentleness of the Mediterranean. Even today I can remember the excitement of that first visit to the cellars. Not just the bracing freshness of that magnificent cellar but the near-mystical feelings provoked by the barrels. Certain walls, I remember, oozed water from a hidden source. There was no doubting the sense of mystery and magic at the heart of L'Hospitalet, and I was suddenly reminded of something my father used to say: "There is no *art de vivre* without wine". As a child I did not understand what he meant. But standing here, in this place known as L'Hospitalet, it suddenly became clear. In the Languedoc, wine is the symbol of hospitality, the basic tenet of *art de vivre*.

Ever since the Middle Ages, people have honoured their guests on their arrival and their departure, and during banquets. Small amounts of wine were consumed with the food, but vast quantities were consumed during toasts to the assembled guests at the beginning and end of the meal. It became a tradition to pass a cup or goblet around the table in re-creation of a ritual beloved in antiquity by the Romans and Greeks. Contemporary etiquette guides decreed: "The cup must be taken with a sign of gratitude, held in both hands, drunk from only lightly to avoid intoxication and then handed onward to your neighbour with one hand only, without spilling a drop. It is important not to directly address someone while they are drinking". The king, for his part, received the goblet once it had been cleaned, filled and tasted by the cup-bearer. This ritual was called the *vin d'honneur,* or the wine of honour. The kings of France offered their guests white wine "as clear as the tears of Christ". Once the meal was over, they put sweet wines into their guests' bedrooms, often alongside biscuits and fruit. The most precious sweet wines came from Frontignan and were served in crystal carafes sealed tight with glass stoppers.

As the centuries passed, the tradition of *vins d'honneurs* during large events such as weddings was slowly forgotten, yet offering the best wines to guests remained a sign of welcome. Be strict with your own wine, as you want to offer the maximum pleasure to your guests; be indulgent with the wine of others, because it is a friend who is offering it to you, wrote Maurice Constantin-Weyer in the *Spirit of Wine*. Around me, as I sat in the restaurant, guests were beginning to take an aperitif. A few were enjoying a bottle accompanied by a plate of thinly sliced salami. Suddenly I said to myself that if I ever had the chance to own this estate, that I would continue these traditions; build on them, and bring their values and those of this land out to a wider audience.

Someone called me over. I was roused from my thoughts, pushed back my chair and greeted a man who I estimated to be around 60 years old, who had a warm and open smile, a healthy complexion and who radiated strength and energy. I took his hand in mine and opened the conversation with, "You are a visionary!"

After lengthy negotiations, I became the new owner on April 1, 2002.

The headquarters of our company moved here, and I kept my promise to build on the work of Jacques Ribourel, pushing everything a little bit further. I adjusted, crafted, and completed what he had begun with such talent and skill. More trees, lavender plants and rose bushes were planted around the landscape.

My main focus at the time, so I believed, was to promote the wines of the South of France and to develop my business. In reality, something extraordinary was happening to me that I had not fully realised when I bought the property–the opportunity to meet the guests who came here. It radically changed my perception. I began to think about everything that I could do to delight our visitors, make them want to return, make them curious to learn more about our approach to wine and to life. I wanted to offer pleasure, quite simply–to offer something enjoyable for the eyes, the palate and the heart.

After this sudden awakening, I asked a team of architects to rework the bedrooms, and I put my wife Ingrid in charge of ensuring that each had its own individual decoration. We named each one after a different one of our estates and chose a colour scheme that was linked to their *terroir*. We set out a bottle of wine from the corresponding château in the bedroom as a gift, alongside two glasses to ensure the gesture was as welcoming as possible. Art became part of the offering. My childhood friend Olivier Domin, who has since gained an international reputation as a painter under the name Olll, set up a workshop in the external courtyard and painted wonderful canvases, some of them to promote the wines. We also renovated the restaurant and ensured there was a wide selection of wines by the glass, allowing visitors to try all our different estates. It still makes me happy to enter the room and see guests animated around a seasonal plate of food, a glass of wine in hand. I feel the warmth of the Mediterranean through these heaping plates of seafood, fresh garden vegetables or Cathar ham.

One evening, as I was wandering around the buildings, letting my mind wander over the day, I was struck by the sense of silence and became aware that there was something missing. Music. Not the harmonious whisper of the wind that breathed through the courtyard, but the langorous "bubble of jazz" so beloved by Toulousain Claude Nougaro.

20

Domaine de l'Aigle

Asking questions

In our profession, regularly questioning established beliefs–even your own–is essential. Sometimes it is necessary to get to the heart of things.

The winemakers of the Haut Vallée de L'Aude had long believed that their *terroir* was not suitable for quality winemaking. For a long time the steep slopes that stretched around the village of Roquetaillade were not allowed to use the name Limoux, despite being only 10 kilometres away from the town. Vines were rare. At this 500-metre altitude, the winemakers would grow the typical Mediterranean varieties of carignan or aramon, but would have a tough time getting them to ripen and were not proud of the results. What they loved to do instead, as night fell across the valley, was watching the eagles circle in the sky above the highest treetops of the region. Those trees, from the foothills of the Pyrénées, dominated what vines they had.

One day, during the 1980s, the local cooperative cellar Sieur d'Arques began a soil study with funding from the regional chamber of agriculture. The slopes revealed a strange richness. In contrast to expectations, the composition of the soil seemed to be more suited to non-native grape varieties than to those typical of the south. Most important, they had potential. Now that there was scientific proof of this, all that was needed was to plant the right grapes. The locals began to realise that just maybe they had underestimated the treasure that they had beneath their feet.

This was the moment that a visionary man arrived. Originally from Champagne, his family had been vine growers for many generations, but Jean-Louis Denois wanted to forge his own path. He left to explore Australia, South America and South Africa and was energised by this contact with winemakers of the New World. When he returned to France, he moved to Roquetaillade with the intention of putting all that he had learnt into practice on French soil. In 1989 Denois bought the highest estate in the village and called it Domaine de L'Aigle–the land of the eagles. He found that he too loved to watch them swoop down from the trees where they had built their nest, refreshed by the air that was more Pyrenean than Mediterranean. Their soaring flight never failed to swell his heart, and it made him want to honour the beauty of the surrounding landscape. Jean-Louis Denois was true to his word and pulled up many of the ancient vines that were growing on his property, replacing them with chardonnay–a plant with large branches, small grapes and a golden colour. This is a grape found most famously in Burgundy and in Champagne, but also in one or two local spots, as it is used in the making of the sparkling Crémant de Limoux.

Here in Roquetaillade, many wondered if it would work and what he was going to do next. In answer to their questions, the young winemaker just jumped right in and his first vintage was a success. He did not produce much, but it was good. Critics responded warmly. He decided to go even further and planted another variety that would just a few years later become immensely famous in the United States thanks to the film *Sideways*, about two buddies on a road trip in California. The noble variety of pinot noir–small compact grapes, blue-black seeds, colourless juice–is used by the greatest estates of Burgundy, elevated by the monks of Citeaux Abbey in the 11th century. Denois' gamble succeeded once again and he produced a delicate, floral wine that was critically acclaimed. Having achieved all that, bizarrely, he sold his estate.

Antonin Rodet, *négociants* and wine producers since 1875, were the next to buy it. This prestigious company, based in the Côte Châlonnaise, was fascinated by the possibilities of Domaine de l'Aigle but after a few years decided that it needed to refocus on its own region. The estate was once again on the market and, as with L'Hospitalet, I received a phone call asking if I was interested. I was not, in theory, looking to buy anything more and yet...after visiting the place, I fell in love. The village itself, with its beautiful old houses, is magnificent, the landscape peaceful in places and dramatic in others. The entire place made me feel at home. I met the passionate and committed estate manager, Vincent Charleux, and we talked. After visiting the 25 hectares of vines that were trained vertically down the slopes, we tasted the wines.

This was 2006. The estate was ready for someone new to take a gamble on it, that much I could feel. I climbed a nearby slope up to the tree line and felt even more convinced that the place would only become even more special as the vines reached maturity. Heading into the cellars, where the equipment was modern and well set out according to the Burgundy model, I could feel the stirrings of a new adventure. Experimenting with pinot and chardonnay at this altitude would allow me to expand not only my range of wines but also my skills. I was ready to take over the baton extended by the former owners who had begun to build up this place, and I was determined to take it ever higher. Our objective was to rival the great chardonnays and pinots of the world, and in 2007 we finally became owners.

Domaine de l'Aigle is the true realisation of precision viticulture. Every single decision is taken only after calling into question all our practices and being certain that what we are doing will lead to the best quality wine. It is not easy to take a step out of your comfort zone and learn new ways of doing things. Everything that I have learned here came with a touch of uncertainty–not least trying to understand an entirely new variety.

Pinot Noir is delicate, fragile, and subtle, both feminine and masculine, yin and yang in one grape. To work pinot noir at altitude is a real delight because it reveals its true nobility in a fresh, continental climate. My ambition was to go beyond simply learning how to work with pinot. I wanted to surpass expectations, to ensure that the variety expressed the *terroir* in a way that did justice to its origins. Charles Rousseau, one of the greatest pinot experts in Gevrey-Chambertin, explained the best way to harvest by saying, "You know, Gérard, when you put pinot noir in your mouth, it needs to sting a bit". It means that, unlike syrah or grenache, the best of pinot is not found by waiting until it has reached the very limit of ripeness, but rather by picking it while it retains some of the freshness and acidity that gives it character.

One year later, in 2008, my colleagues and I decided to put ourselves to the test and submit the wine to the Mondial des Pinots, the yearly international competition of the grape held in Switzerland. Over 1,000 wines are tasted by a panel of internationally renowned experts. We sent our samples, waited and... surprise. The 2007 vintage of Domaine de l'Aigle had been placed in front of pinots from countries all over the world and had won the highest distinction–the Grand Or. We had produced a great pinot noir.

That day, happy and moved, I went to the estate and followed the path up to the small lake that marks the farthest extent of our vineyard. I looked up to the skies, where the eagles were on the hunt. My heart swelled in gratitude at the recognition that this place had been given, and any remaining doubts that I had were swept away. Our risk had paid off and we were on the right track.

21

Château Aigues-Vives

The four elements

The landscape of the Languedoc is punctuated by vineyards, *garrigue*, streams and rivers, abbeys and châteaux. More mysteriously, ancient springs have left their imprint on certain parts of this land. Their influence is seen in the names of two abbeys, Fontfroide and Fontcaude–"cold fountain" and "warm fountain"–recognising the sacred dimension of water. It is essential to life and yet can be relegated to the status of a simple bodily need. In fact it is the majority component of both earth and man. And we sometimes forget that one third of the planet lacks access to clean drinking water.

Water is also an essential component of wine. It has a particularly important role in biodynamics because dynamised water–water charged by cosmic energy by a special stirring technique that creates a vortex–is used in the pulverization of plant extracts that will then be spread in the vineyards several times a year. Water and wine each possess a different vibratory frequency, and it is possible to talk of the wave that flows within wine.

Aigues-Vives means "living waters" or "water of life". A living water is one that is dynamised. You simply have to experience the difference between drinking water out of a plastic bottle and from a flowing stream to realise that a single sip can quench the thirst with the latter, and an entire bottle is barely enough with the former.

We have found numerous ancient Roman thermal springs around this château, which we bought in 2010.

The Barsalou family was the original owner of this estate, and they adhered to the traditional farming practices of Corbières. It was then bought by the Bordeaux merchant house Dourthe in the 1990s, which was entranced by its remote location and the significant volume of wine that it produces. They renovated the vines and the cellars with precision and skill, and we are thrilled to benefit from their preparatory work. We also benefit from the location of the vines, which lie right next to those of Domaine de Villemajou while having a separate identity all their own.

We are here in the heart of Corbières, on the best *terroirs* of the Boutenac region. The soils are laid out across ancient flint-filled terraces that transmit bursts of minerality to the wine. The blend of old carignan, syrah, grenache and mourvèdre combine to reveal the originality and beauty of Château Aigues-Vives. The vats are laid out in connecting rooms along a single axis in the renovated wine cellar, as is traditional in the South of France, and the wines are aged in a spectacular barrel cellar. This theatrical place is reminiscent of some Bordeaux châteaux and was created at the end of the 1990s as a continuation of the vinification cellars. The line of barrels stretches away in front of you, amplifying the sense of space.

The soul of Aigues-Vives is both peaceful and harmonious. Centuries-old trees, with a poplar that stretches 25 metres high, grow in the park that surrounds the property, giving perspective and humility. The newly landscaped approach has emphasised the contours of the vineyard, giving a feeling of being rooted in its landscape and its *terroir*.

Even though the two estates are neighbours, the personalities of Aigues-Vives and Villemajou are truly distinct. Here the freshness of the fruit is paramount, while Villemajou is perhaps a little more expressive and sophisticated. The alchemy of the blend, the different proportion of grapes used, takes us on a journey to two separate worlds. Our role is to understand the personality of each place and to help the wine to best express its own character.

22

Château La Sauvageonne

In harmony with nature

As I walk across the plateau of Larzac, I am reminded of the brave fight that took place for this land, when local landowners resisted the extension of a military base here in the 1970s, preserving instead the original character of the landscape. José Bové was among the key figures of this non-violent action, which became part of the anti-globalisation fight, and which left a lasting imprint on the soul of the area. It marked me at the time because, in the early 1980s, my sister Guylaine and I were here on a caving trip near Millau. Larzac is a stunning place; wild, sprawling, arid, perfectly suited to the open-air grazing of the brébis sheep from whose milk comes Roquefort cheese–a national treasure even among the dizzying array of French cheeses. Toward the south of the region the *terroir* takes the name of the Terrasses de Larzac. Here a rich geological history imbues Lodève, Saint-Jean-de-La-Blaquière, Saint-Félix-de-Lodez and the lake of Salagou with a special force and character. Ever since my first visit, I have been struck by the contrasting colours and textures of the soil, the grandiose impact of the volcanic landscape, and the rich, unspoiled proximity of nature.

Previous owners have all left their own imprint–the composed Englishman Fred Brown who took over from Gaetan Poncé, the first to reveal the potential of this estate by creating two separate cuvées representing the two distinct *terroirs* that are found here.

The first is made up of "ruffe" rocks comprised of red volcanic rock rich in iron oxide that change colour depending on the time of day and the reflection of the sun's rays. I asked my friend and photographer Yann Arthus-Bertrand to photograph the wild moonscape of this place, where the soils mark the grapes, particularly syrah and grenache, with a verticality and gripping minerality. The high Larzac plateau means regular rain in August, allowing the grapes to develop perfectly, with a brief respite from the high temperatures and arid summer heat.

The lake of Salagou, created in the 1960s, is a hymn to what humanity can achieve. A vast stretch of water, an ode to beauty and biodiversity, overwhelming and ever-changing depending on the reflections of clouds fleeing across the water and the elongated patterns they cast on the volcanic soils. Just a few metres away, the schist slopes of the hills rise in contrasting strips of red brick soils and basalt black rocks. The array of different shapes, from tiny fragments of sandstone to small round pebbles to rectangular-shaped flint, produces wines of startling originality; with a little imagination we can imagine here that we are producing a symphony from the schist. After two years of careful observation and tasting, we decided to create one wine that would blend the complementary characteristics of each *terroir*. The marriage of the two has created a wine of power and complexity, a benediction of this legendary site.

We also produce a smaller amount of an excellent white wine that comes solely from the schist soils, comprised of vermentino, roussanne, grenache blanc and viognier grapes. Alongside these we make use of the fresh character of the cinsault, complemented by the elegance of grenache, to make a precise, lilting rosé.

Fred Brown had the happy idea of building a wonderful country house above the cellar and winery. His aim was to build in an elevated location in order to benefit from the astonishing views, and so he enlisted the services of his daughter, an architect in Los Angeles.

Legend has it that she was too busy to travel back and forth to her father's Languedoc estate so she simply sent him the plans for Joan Collins's house and advised him to build the same. A Californian influence perhaps, but the house was built from local stone and France's honour remained intact. We never cease to be astonished by the beauty of this place. Time stands still here–particularly when sharing food, wine and the view with a group of good friends.

We recently received a strange visitor while drinking a glass of white wine next to the pool. A Griffon vulture with a wingspan of perhaps 2.5 metres plummeted down right in front of us. After recovering from the astonishment, we rushed to get it out of the water to prevent it from drowning. Not an easy task considering the size of the bird. Once safely out, it lay dazed and sleeping for two hours until representatives from the Society for the Protection of Birds arrived. This dedicated group took care of the vulture for the next two months and nursed it back to health. Eventually it could fly again and returned to the wild; an incredible event that once again strengthened our commitment to biodiversity across all of our properties and reminded us that nature is both our heritage and the future of humanity.

23

Château La Soujeole

Channeling energy

When you leave the main road between Carcassonne and Limoux, Château La Soujeole appears to your right after a couple of bends, nestled down in the landscape just outside the village of Montclar. It is a place that inspires the deepest existential questions. How do we give meaning to our lives? What path am I meant to follow to be true to who I am? How do we let go of our egos and simply listen to the vibrations of our spirit? If we allow the sense of calm and silence that reigns here to truly wash over us, the answers start to reveal themselves. I met the Monseigneur de la Soujeole over 10 years ago. He was looking after his family wine estate while also continuing his ecclesiastical duties as a bishop, spreading the church's teachings and fulfilling his commitment to God. He saw his commitment to this landscape as another mission that brought him closer to the rhythm of the seasons, to the state of grace of the countryside and the men and women whose souls have shaped it over the years. When I met his mother, Marie Antoinette, I could understand his visceral attachment to this château, with its unshakeable bonds to his own family history. This 92-year-old woman was still full of vitality and warmth, an embodiment of the power and strength of positive thought that defies the passing of the years. This was a woman of rare spirit who was fully engaged with the world, with sharp eyes that missed nothing. Her son Bertrand was sharing a part of her life in this place with her, and it clearly nourished them both.

When Monseigneur asked me to take over the running of the property, following several years when I had been selling a part of the production, I brought along my estate director to undertake an in-depth visit of the surrounding landscape. That was the day that I first appreciated the soul of the Malepère appellation; a name that means "bad stones" even though these same rocks partially built the majestic city of Carcassonne. The countryside here is gently picturesque, with valleys and softly rising slopes. The climate is a combination of Mediterranean heat and a cooler oceanic influence from the west, supplying the perfect combination of freshness and warmth that allows a full but gentle ripening of grapes.

I have always loved the finesse, structure and singular personality of cabernet franc. When blended with merlot or malbec it takes on both delicacy and complexity, with a balance and aromatic finesse that, when combined with slow aging, is the signature of truly great wines. By keeping yields low, we are able to produce an exceptional wine at Château La Soujeole. The myriad exposures of the vines means that harvest is almost always stretched out over several weeks allowing each grape, in each different spot, to reach its perfect level of ripeness.

Between Narbonne and Limoux, the Aude department marks the passage between the semi-arid Mediterranean climate and the softer oceanic climate of southwestern France. It has long been known for its unusual ecology, the wide variety of wild herbs such as thyme, rosemary and lavender, and the exceptional quality of its forests. All of these things vibrate through the wines of Château La Soujeole–freshness, density, texture, complexity, and the alchemy of cabernet franc, malbec and merlot.

Malepère is also the closest vineyard to Castelnaudary, the world capital of cassoulet, one of the most beloved dishes in France. Ever since childhood I have delighted in this slow-cooked dish of white beans, duck or goose *confit*, offal and Toulouse sausage–an important ingredient that anchors the dish to the ancient capital of Occitan. Three chefs are particularly renowned for their rendition of this local gastronomic cult. First, in Comte Roger restaurant in Carcassonne, Pierre Mesa uses both duck and goose *confit* in his recipe, and enjoying it among the haunting beauty of the Carcassonne citadel anchors me to my Languedoc roots. I also love the more classical, traditional cassoulet prepared by Jean-Claude Rodriguez at Château Saint-Martin-de-Trencavel, and I admire his promotion of the dish through the Grand Confrérie de Cassoulet. Finally, I reserve a particular attachment to the version prepared by my friend André Pachon, the King of Cassoulet in Tokyo. He has achieved the spectacular feat of sharing this humble representation of our *art de vivre* with the imperial family of Japan. As you would expect, the wines of Malepère and of Château La Soujeole work perfectly alongside a hearty plate of cassoulet, but they work equally well alongside more delicate dishes, notably those based on beef.

Developing the reputation of this appellation in France and farther afield has been a great joy to me. To be able to contribute in a small way to uncovering the ambition of a magnificent *terroir* that deserves to be more widely known, and to create a new star in the galaxy of premium French wines, is something of a tiny miracle, and I am grateful to be a part of it.

24

Château des Karantes

A Celebration of the Mediterranean

Lying just behind Narbonne-Plage in a small valley overlooking the Mediterranean Sea, at the heart of La Clape in the Narbonne national park, Château des Karantes is a haven of peace. The vineyard is named after a former owner and Bishop of Carcassonne.

Just over a decade ago, in the early 2000s, the Knysz family from Detroit, Michigan, bought the property and strengthened the long-held connection between the South of France and American wine lovers. Walter Knysz, his wife Janet, and their sons Walter and Jason committed themselves to this splendid property that is surrounded on three sides by steep cliffs, a protected enclave in La Clape sheltered from the harsh north winds. The 43 hectares of vines stretch along the clay-limestone soils of the valley, lending powerful aromatic character to the highly prized red and white wines.

The white wines are made up of a majority of bourboulenc, an indigenous grape known for its long growing cycle and strong personality. To this is added an unusual and subtle blend of grenache, roussanne, vermentino and old vine terret blanc, planted in 1927. The minerality drawn from the limestone rocks reinforces a sense of lightness and gives the wine a long aging ability. The saline character and clean fruit provides a link to the character of the estate's red wines, which are made from the traditional local marriage of syrah, grenache, mourvèdre and carignan.

Its proximity to Château L'Hospitalet and a decisive meeting with Walter led to us joining together to breathe new life into Château des Karantes and its exceptional wine. The natural power and energy of the place made an instant impression on me, as did the commitment of the Knysz family, who trusted me to take the wine to the next level. To achieve this, we carried out a precise geological study of the vineyard and its surrounding environment, where the limestone rocks blended with the Mediterranean *garrigue*. I knew there was the same potential for greatness here as with Château L'Hospitalet, and we began to set out a plan for revealing the essence of this stunning *terroir* that benefits from the gentle sea breezes from the fine, long sandy beaches of Narbonne-Plage and Saint-Pierre-la-Mer. We are currently focusing on restoring the buildings to create a place to welcome and nurture lovers of nature and biodiversity.

Standing here, it is easy to understand why the Romans chose to make this their home and to call it Narbonnaise in honour of Narbo Martius, the first daughter of Rome. Being here deepens our understanding of our cultural heritage and history. The remoteness of La Clape is its great strength; reinforcing the character of its biotope, its wildlife and also its destiny as a place of welcome and *art de vivre*. Here, also, we have taken the decision to introduce biodynamic farming practices, in line with our philosophy, to reinforce the varietal origins and character of these wines. It is a new challenge for our team and a commitment to deepening our footprint within the exceptional La Clape appellation.

The adventure of taking this wonderful appellation forward is shared with the winemakers of Châteaux Rouquette-sur-Mer; d'Angles; Moujan; Mire-l'Étang; Capitoul; les Monges; La Negly; Camplazens; Tarailhan; Pech-Redon and my closest neighbours at Mas du Soleilla, and all the others who are working toward the establishment and recognition of a land that pushes us toward excellence and brings out the best in all of us.

History is repeating itself here, as we want to share this place with all those who love our heritage and lifestyle. United by the same ambition, we are participating in the renewal of the Languedoc, worthy successors to the conquering Romans who first joined hands together with people and races on all sides of our beloved Mediterranean Sea.

III

THE TERROIRS

25

La Forge

Making a difference

The guiding force behind all our actions is the desire to find meaning in our lives, in our work and in everything we do. Sometimes it takes one word to make things clear, but more usually getting to the heart of things is a slow process of reflection and discovery.

October 1997. My flight from Paris to Montpellier had just landed, and I finally knew what I was going to do next. It had taken me 10 years of searching, of returning to the question during moments of calm, or in the quiet space as I was falling asleep–how was I going to properly honour my father's life? Often air travel allows us moments where our thoughts are free to wander, for our minds to climb up to the heavens while our bodies, seated and still, simply rest. For a few minutes I sat staring at the wings as we passed over the clouds. I felt good, and my thoughts began to take shape. October is the traditional month for me to take stock. I had followed the path set out by my father. I had truly committed to a life in wine, as a vine grower, a winemaker and a *négociant*. I did my best to lead by example and focus on quality, even if there were inevitably some failures that came either from impatience or lack of experience. I was starting to feel that I had turned a corner, most notably in my skills as a winemaker. I could feel that I was reaching a new level of finesse and precision that, I knew all too well, was the key to the elusive quality of great wine. My father would have been proud, and I would have loved for him to taste the wines that I was producing.

As I was thinking all of this, a clear image suddenly appeared in my mind of my father walking in his favourite spot at Villemajou. It was a plot of vines called La Forge, so-named because there was once an iron forger there. He was walking freely among the vines, touching the shoots with his hands, as I had seen him do many times. And then he turned around and walked softly up to me, as if in a dream, and looked deep into my eyes. For a moment, the intensity of his gaze unnerved me. I felt like I could read my future in it. And then he disappeared, swallowed up by my shock.

When the plane landed it was nighttime, and the lights below were gently winking. I could see Montpellier shining below us, some sections humming with life, others shaded and darkened. I finally knew what I had to do. I would vinify La Forge, my father's favourite plot of vines, as a separate wine. And I would make it something exceptional; a blend of 100-year old carignan, that tasted as if the blood of the earth flowed through it, with our oldest syrah.

The first vintage of La Forge was born in 1998.

It has become a blend like no other, an alchemy of vine, *terroir* and of all the lessons that I have learnt thus far. It represents the spirit of Georges Bertrand.

26

Le Viala

Following your instinct

Sometimes an object arrives that is so laden with significance that we have no option but to follow where it leads, however unexpected. This has happened twice in my life. Being able to follow your instincts means accepting that coincidences are sometimes signs of the magic that is within us and our universe.

It was 7.30 in the morning, but the sun was already rising. Fairly normal for a midsummer day, June 23, the day before the Fête de la Saint Jean. I had decided to take an early tour of my vines at La Livinière and was wandering slowly between the rows of one of our highest plots, up at 250 metres in altitude, enjoying the last traces of freshness of a day that was clearly shaping up to be steaming. Birds were singing their morning chorus, the sky was cloudless. I had just reached a path bordered by a dry stone wall when I looked up toward the church that stood a few hundred metres from me on the horizon. Two rays of the morning sun shone from behind its minaret-shaped bell tower, illuminating a few row of vines to the right of where I was standing. It looked biblical, so concentrated were the rays of light. Clearly the light was shining through the tower's two windows, but how had the sun climbed so high by this hour of the morning? Or was it just a reflection? I hardly stopped to consider an answer; I simply rejoiced in the moment. Maybe I was a witness to something magical, to a moment of grace that was taking place at this particular spot on this particular midsummer morning. Sometimes the very familiarity of a place means that we ignore its potential. This was a plot called Le Viala, just in front of La Lavinière village. Its name comes from the Latin *cella vinaria*, meaning "wine cellar", because it was the Romans who had first cultivated vines on this spot. I made a note of it, then turned to the tasks of the day, tucking away this mysterious occurrence in my mind, not really sure of its significance.

A few months later, once the harvest of all the separate plots of Laville-Bertrou was finished, we began to prepare for our blending sessions. Once again my colleagues and I retired to our "temple" to work, searching out the perfect blend with the same sense of commitment and pleasure as ever. Among the 30 bottles set up along the work surface I came across three, each a different grape variety, all labeled "Viala". Out of simple curiosity, I decided to blend all three and taste them together.

I could feel a strange mix of impatience and hope as I did so, as if something extraordinary was happening. As I brought the glass to my lips, I immediately felt the power of the blend–a stunning marriage of syrah, grenache and carignan. It was not yet perfect, but I continued to search, to refine, to find the keys to unlocking the nirvana that I was certain was waiting. I inched toward a wine that was structured, muscular, full-fleshed, powerful. There were moments when it slipped out of reach until I finally said, "I think I have it, will someone taste?"

As is always the case when a blend is successful, we were united in our agreement. "What are we going to call it?" asked one of my colleagues. The answer was clear. This was Le Viala.

It was only later, when looking out the window in my office, that I remembered the events of that June morning. Those three ancient varieties had combined to transmit the same sense of freshness, power and beauty that I had felt in the vineyard, the night before the Fête de la Saint Jean–John the Baptist. Everything became clear. The light that I had seen in the vines was a sign showing me the path to this particular wine. Le Viala had been drawn into existence by the rays of the sun.

27

L'Hospitalitas

Taking pride in our roots

There is a great strength in being proud of your country, of your family, of your childhood, and of having respect for your ancestors. To be proud of where you come from means that you have a solid base for spreading your wings, heading out into the world and sharing your truth. Our roots are a source of power for each and every one of us.

"We are winemakers born in a region where life is blessed", my father wrote in a letter to his team of vine growers in January 1980. "A region that since the earliest times has been influenced by the civilisation of the vine and the veneration of the bulldeity Apis. We are fortunate to cultivate lands that nourish us with the many contrasting moods of mountain, *garrigue*, plains, lakes and sea".

At his funeral, just as he was being returned to the earth, I saw his childhood friend and school classmate, the historian Jacques Michaud. This was a man who had been very close to my father, and yet this was the first time that I had met him. Approaching me at a moment that is always profoundly upsetting and disturbing, the words he chose not only gave me strength, but also helped me to focus on how I was going to move forward.

When I bought Château L'Hospitalet, it was Jacques who came up with the perfect adage to sum up what we wanted to achieve here. Ever the Latin scholar, he suggested *Sine vino vana hospitalitas*–"There is no hospitality without wine". Soon after, I decided to select a specific plot of vines to create a cuvée in honour of my birthplace Narbonne and its charitable religious order that was once known as the *Hospitalet*–a wine that would celebrate hospitality and generosity in all its forms. Narbonne can trace its origins back to the Romans. It was founded in 118 BC by a Senate decree creating a port on the shores of the Mediterranean and with it the oldest Roman colony on French soil; *colonia Narbo Martius*. Just over half a century later, in 49 BC, Narbonne overtook Marseille as the main stopping-off point between Spain and Italy. It was the main centre for exporting oil, wood, hemp, plant tinctures and wild herbs, cheeses, butter, cattle...and wine. In return, the Romans sent marble and pottery to Narbonne, which was used to build many of the sumptuous buildings that line the city today.

"A boulevard to the glory of Rome", wrote Ciceron of Narbonne. "The most beautiful", said Martial, who considered it the capital of this Roman province. When the Visigoths sacked Rome in 410 AD, they claimed Narbonne as their capital. In 800 AD, under Charlemagne, Narbonne again became a capital city for the Duchy of the Goths. The city continued to grow in wealth and importance until the 17th century, when the surrounding land silted up and encircled the city, cutting it off from the sea. Its soul and spirit could have been extinguished by the loss of its port, but instead it was nourished by its viticultural richness. Narbonne remained the uncontested capital of the local wine industry, and its wine merchants continued to do fine business.

Beyond its history with wine, Narbonne was a place of welcome. It is worth remembering that in the 15th century, when the Hospitalet was founded, the building was not–even though its name may suggest it–used as a hospital. An *hospitalet* was rather a place of rest, a refuge for the poor. It was a place to interact with others and to be replenished. The same notion is found in the etymology of the Latin word *hospitalitas*, which signified–in the years before the arrival of Christianity–sharing a region between its indigenous people and their Roman conquerors. It was this notion of sharing, duly introduced by the Romans, that allowed all of the ancient world to live alongside each other peacefully, the Romans just as much as the Gauls. In recognition of this history, this cuvée is made to honour Narbonne's ancient roots that saw generosity and sharing as the best way for different cultures to exist alongside each other.

L'Hospitalitas is a plot of three hectares set in a magical hollow, well shaded and bordered by truffle trees, a field of mulberry bushes and an old olive grove. Syrah, blended with a few touches of mourvèdre, exhales black fruits, the scents and tastes of the Mediterranean and, as it ages, black truffles. The story of all that passed here seems to flow through these vines, and they deserve the chance to share their history and that of Narbonne. I simply helped them to sing of this land that we love.

I was born in Narbonne, where I had the great fortune to grow up as part of a large and happy family. Since earliest childhood I knew its vines as deeply as I knew myself, and my roots are entwined in its rocky soils. The tang of sea salt carried by the wind still tastes of my childhood, and when cicadas sing I can close my eyes and be back at home. The *art de vivre* that I live by today comes from deep within.

28

L'Aigle Royal

Keeping the faith

"I say to you today, my friends, even though we face the difficulties of today and tomorrow, I still have a dream".

– Martin Luther King, on the steps of the Lincoln Memorial, Washington D.C., August 28, 1963.

What are golden eagles–*les aigles royals* in French–looking at as they take flight? Their prey, certainly. But do they also take in the beauty of this landscape, where chardonnay and pinot vines take root 500 metres above sea level, on south-facing slopes where a path meanders slowly upwards toward a wine estate, past sunflowers and the village of Roquetaillade, with its church and its château below? Do they watch us as we break eagerly into a run as we climb the hill? Can they feel us overcome by the beauty of this place, our lungs full of the purity of the air, replenishing our souls? I often wonder, and so have named this wine, which comes from our highest plot of chardonnay vines and produces a voluptuous wine of soaring acidity, L'Aigle Royal in honour of the pair of majestic, noble and faithful golden eagles that fly over Domaine de L'Aigle. Tradition would have it that the birth of the chardonnay grape was in Burgundy, but scholars believe that its true origins lie closer to the hills above Jerusalem. Even the origin of the word chardonnay has its roots in the Bible; a translation of the Hebrew *cha'ar adon'ai*, or "the gate of God". The first crusaders, on their return from the Middle East, planted the variety in France, from where it was brought to the Cistercian monks in Burgundy. This knowledge reinforces our belief in the great potential of the hillside *terroirs* of the Mediterranean for the noblest grape varieties. Pinot noir itself almost certainly comes from Burgundy–grown by the Gauls and taking its name from the pinecone shape of its grape clusters.

I consider this history as I watch the birds in flight. Eagles soar high above the earth and yet they always keep their eyes on the earth. They remind me of the words of Antoine de Saint-Exupéry: "Make your life a dream, and the dream a reality". Realising a dream takes time and hard work and, when you achieve it, the feeling is incomparable. I, too, have a dream. And when I walk up to these vines and stand staring into the face of nature, I confide my dream to the heavens and ask them to give me the strength to realise it.

In recent years I have begun to live my dream for this highest corner of Domaine de l'Aigle, where we have now added pinot noir alongside the chardonnay vines. Standing among the vines of L'Aigle Royal, I can today turn to the mountains that vibrate with the spirit of the Cathars and give thanks for the dream that is now made real, brought to life through tasting the fruit of two plots, one red, one white, that uncover the essence and stunning complexity of two noble grapes.

The chardonnay, after up to eight months of aging in oak barrels, attains complexity, richness and minerality that ensures a long life to come. Pinot, which has taught me so much about precision and minimalism, here shows exactly why it is a grape so lauded for its expression of *terroir*, its ability to touch emotions, to transmit a message, and to send out an invitation to spirituality.

Bottled in magnums, both of these wines will continue to confer their messages on wine lovers for many decades to come.

IV

BACK TO THE FUTURE

29

Tautavel

Revealing the soul of a terroir

Revealing the soul of a *terroir* means shining a light on that which is hidden. Nature is nothing without the work of man, and it takes many men to work a vineyard. Each supports the other, and it is the collective belief of a whole team that allows a wine to fully reveal its true nature. On July 22, 1961, 36-year-old architect Henry de Lumley discovered a human skull in a small cave hollowed out of a mountain, overlooking a valley known as the Caune de l'Arago.

Over the next 40 years, Lumley and his team succeeded in uncovering over 120 human fossils in the Arago Cave and many other places. Those remains belonged to humans who had lived between 690,000 and 300,000 years ago. Thanks to their work, carried out for seven months of every year for 40 years, humanity has been able to catch a glimpse of Tautavel Man, one of the oldest examples of *homo erectus* in Europe, thought to be 450,000 years old. The village of Tautavel was changed by the discovery also, warmly welcoming visitors drawn by the fame of the cave and the subsequent museum and research centre that are located there.

It was a far earlier discovery of prehistoric animal bones at this spot–by geologist and professor Marcel de Serras in 1836–that led to the uncovering, 125 years later, of our earliest ancestors. And the local villagers played their part also, embracing the new life that had been offered to them by the incredible treasures that their landscape contained.

I have always liked the village of Tautavel, located in the foothills of the High Pyrénées where a limestone plateau forms a chalk circle. Its traditional village houses have the feel of mountain retreats despite their roofs being covered with the red tiles of the Mediterranean. I have had many happy times here. It is easy to understand what attracted prehistoric man to this magnificent landscape when walking across the limestone plateau that lies above the village. The caves would have afforded an endless view of the Verdouble valley–highly useful for watching the peaceful grazing of bighorn sheep, deer, rhinoceroses and buffalo while preparing for a hunt. These early hunters are thought to have used the cave sometimes as a permanent home, and other times as a seasonal base for tracking animals in an arc of around 30 kilometres.

The vines would have first colonized the landscape around the 6th century BC, as man tirelessly continued his quest to cultivate, procreate, and claim new territories as his own. And as this quest continues, the turbulence of our more recent history becomes increasingly disturbing. Yann Arthus-Bertrand has captured its truth in his film *Home*, making clear the challenges that we face in protecting our planet. He takes key dates–the formation of the earth between 4 million and 600 million years ago, the appearance of the first bacterial life forms between 3 billion and 500 million years ago, the arrival of man 4 million years ago and that of Tautavel man 450,000 years ago–and sets those milestones against the 100 years that have elapsed since the Industrial Revolution. A blink of an eye that is threatening the survival of the planet and all those who live on it.

As we hurtle forward ever faster to a time radically different from that of our ancestors, our minds and bodies inevitably find it bewildering to metabolise these rapid changes. To even attempt to make sense of the changes, we need to study Tautavel–to return to the source of humanity and to understand that we are insignificant and allow that knowledge to bring us comfort. I like to stand on the plateau above Tautaval and admire the form of the natural limestone that encircles it. I like to enjoy the shapes of the vineyards that stretch away below me. I know Tautavel's power. Tautavel is a wonderful *terroir* that is translated through the grenache noir, carignan and syrah that grow upon it. It is the very paucity of these soils that is the source of its power. Meagre schist abounds and forces the roots of the vines to reach down deep into the earth. It is in the balance between that which is visible–the plant, the leaves, the fruit–and that which is invisible–its deep root system burrowing down through the rocks in the hunt for the slightest hint of water–that the vine finds its best expression.

At Tautavel, everything comes from within, just as warmth and generosity are intrinsically contained within wine. But in wine as with the caves of Tautavel, it is not just the land itself that should be honoured but the men who have uncovered its truth. In Tautavel, these were Joseph Monzo, Régis Ougères and the oenologist Marcel Rouillé. When I arrived here for the first time in 1995, it was to meet with a group of winemakers who were ready to work together to create a new range of wines. They believed, as I do, that wine here has a particular character because of the richness of the site's history, the tangible link that it represents between the many generations that have stood on this earth, and because of the remarkable character that it teases out of the grenache grape. These soils, by turns schist and limestone, seem to draw different conversations out of this grape that see it grow, by turn, black, grey and white–noir, gris and blanc.

Grenache noir, the dominant component of any blend from the Tautavel appellation, is a hardy variety that resists drought and transmits a generosity and texture to a wine, alongside a swirling cauldron of brambly and autumnal fruits. The grenache gris, once used for *vins doux naturels*, is today used to make our famous rosé Gris Blanc. And finally the grenache blanc, harvested while it is still fresh, gives a fruity, zest-filled white, racy and lively, that we call *vin vert*.

For blending the Tautavel red cuvées Réserve and Grand Terroir, we ensure a blend of 70 percent grenache noir, 20 percent syrah and 10 percent old carignan. In contrast, the cuvée Hommage, dedicated to the glory of these winemakers, is a selection of only the oldest vines of grenache, many of which have grown on this spot for more than a century.

We quickly agreed on an initial engagement for 10 years with this group of winemakers, and have just renewed it for a second time. Discussions and interactions along the way have strengthened our relationships. We are all driven by the sincere belief that Tautavel has something important to share with the world. It is a project that we work on together, and the improvements are clear with every passing vintage. The heart of this project is the unshakeable bond between the winemakers of the three villages of the Tautavel plateau and my team. We are all proud to be selling the wines in 30 countries–with each bottle contributing to the revelation of the history of the Catalan region and the inheritance that was passed down to us by our ancestors.

30

Gris Blanc, Gio and Code Rouge

The little treasures

Accompanying my love for each of my estates, with their myriad personalities, is the visceral need that I have always felt to create and innovate. It was this need that took me into the Roussillon and more specifically into the Agly Valley, where I was convinced that I could find a new expression of grenache gris among the magnificent contours of the Catalan landscape. Here I found old vines that had long been used as the base for *vins doux naturels*, and most famously Rivesaltes. And yet regular consumption of this style of wine has long been falling steadily in France, and has never really found its place overseas, where it is often left aside in favour of port or sherry.

I discussed this with the president of the Tautavel cooperative cellar and in 2005 experimented with making 6,500 bottles of this new style of wine. The results were better than I could ever have imagined, and we launched it on the market. Intuition led me to calling it Gris Blanc, because the grenache gris could be used in both white and rosé wines. Its crystalline colour, its strong sense of individuality and its singing minerality ensured that it stood out from the countless rosés on the market. Its persistency of flavour and its slightly bitter finish is something that I have always loved. From the second year of production, we began making 40,000 bottles that we began to sell outside of France. Very quickly, over 50 countries had been seduced by the thirst-quenching savoury quality of this wine. The slim bottle and simple, refined label were easily recognisable and helped consumers to take it to their hearts. We are very proud of what we have achieved with Gris Blanc and for rolling out an entirely new product.

The consumption of rosé continues to grow as modern drinkers, and particularly women, find wines to reflect their own lifestyles and that offer immediate pleasure for sharing with friends. Gris Blanc is all about enjoyment and celebrations.

Gio was the childhood nickname of my father Georges. It makes me think of both the rich flavours of the Mediterranean and also a certain cheekiness and desire for freedom. Mediterranean viticulture is indistinguishable from the character of grenache, its principal grape variety–powerful, generous and ripe whether red, white or rosé. My team wanted to create a range of everyday wines that would celebrate this, showcasing its fruit and generosity. These single-variety wines come from the young vines of our region. My father once said to me, "You know Gérard it's difficult to make a bad wine with grenache because it is so perfectly adapted to the weather and landscape of our region". These three wines are proof of those words–a guarantee of pleasure, offered in the spirit of sharing.

From 1990, following the suggestion of Gérard Margeon, sommelier for the Alain Ducasse group, we also developed a range of different bottles for our rosés, notably magnums and jéroboams, to ensure that they would be ever more adapted to showcasing our philosophy of sharing.

A short time later, while nursing an old rum in the bar of Belle Mare hotel in Mauritius, I was suddenly struck by an idea. Without any particular reason, my eye was drawn toward a bottle of vodka, globally recognised thanks to its red label. The eventual launch of Code Red can be dated from this moment. I had always loved sparkling wines, and particularly the great champagnes, and the pleasure and anticipation that they provoke. Opening a bottle of Champagne is a sign of celebration like no other. Always a lover of Dom Pérignon, I had also learnt to appreciate great cuvées of Laurent Perrier, Veuve Clicquot and Nicolas Feuillatte.

New regions have been having increasing success in meeting growing consumer demand for this style of wine. In Limoux, we were ironically held back in the 1990s by the weight of our history with the Blanquette de Limoux. In more recent years, the local cooperative cellars like the Sieur d'Arques along with several excellent producers such as Antech, Denoit and Rosier have begun to experiment with some excellent bottles of sparkling *crémant* that were more than capable of holding their own alongside the best.

I decided to join them and to create a *blanc de blancs* of the highest quality. I turned to Philippe Coulon for advice, not only a great specialist but also a former rugby player. The resulting wine was a blend of chardonnay, chenin and a touch of mauzac and was launched on the market in 2010 under the name Code Rouge. This *crémant de Limoux* is produced in limited quantities to both round out our range of wines and to demonstrate on honest commitment to meeting the needs of our consumers.

We wanted to give it an image that was both surprising and transgressive, because the spirit and the destiny of this product lay in it appealing to consumers who wanted to break the rules and to find their own way in life, pushing their boundaries as I have done so many times. So far, the signs for Code Rouge are promising; after the three years of aging needed to attain the right maturity and complexity, we have successfully launched it onto the market. It is resolutely *haut de gamme*, intended as a mark of respect to one of the key moments in the history of the Languedoc when the monks of Saint Hilaire Abbey, in 1531, created the world's first sparkling wine.

31

Legendary Vintages

Leaving Something Behind

The *terroir* of Roussillon contains numerous secrets and treasures. From them we take our strength, roots, culture and spirituality. The Egyptians, the Israelites, the Greeks, the Romans and later the Visigoths, Cathars and Persians all carry within them traces of the three monotheistic religions of southern Europe, Africa and the Middle East. Our symbols, customs and rituals are rooted in this heritage, developed over thousands of years.

Narbonne was a hugely powerful port in antiquity, second only to Rome. All kinds of exchanges took place on its shores, not least the commerce of wine–first in earthenware jars, then in barrels and finally in large containers. The 1960s saw a rapid growth of viticultural exchanges between France, Spain, Italy and Algeria, all rushing to meet the growing consumer demand for rich, generous wines to quench the thirst of the masses.

Fortified sweet wines such as the *vins doux naturels* always had their own musicality. Their moment of glory stretches back to King Louis XIII, when the French king and his Cardinal Richelieu delighted in the muscats of Frontignan, the most reputed in their eyes.

In the Catalan regions, *vins doux naturels* played an important economic role. The Byrrh family was at the heart of the growth of viticulture in the region in the 1960s by guaranteeing that they would take large quantities of wine to first create a restorative medicine and later an apéritif. They built large wine cellars all over the region for the production and cellaring of their products. In the 1960s, Byrrh was the most popular apéritif in France, with the great advantage that it could be stored pretty much indefinitely. Its sweet taste, silky texture and aromas of oak, fruits and spices gave it wide appeal. It was a style that also perfectly matched some of the traditional sweet treats of the region–the crunchy *croquants* almond biscuits of Saint-Paul-de-Fenouillet, the sugar-dusted *rousquilles* doughnuts that were always best from the bakery in Arles-sur-Tech, made according to a jealously guarded recipe.

In the years following World War II, a few talented winemakers began to sell their own fortified wines, slowly casting off the shackles of the all-powerful merchants. Among the pioneers of rising quality were Mas Amiel, Domaine de Volontat, winemakers of La Côte Radieuse and the Cazes brothers. Three appellations stood out–Rivesaltes, Maury and Banyuls, carving out an identity and pointing to the regional typicity of certain blends.

Maury is the kingdom of grenache noir, the epicentre of the purity and simplicity of this grape. At its best, grenache noir is laden with rich fruits, both elegant and suave. It can be drunk young but also has a remarkable capacity to improve with age. Maury is the brute force, the pride of Roussillon.

Banyuls are almost entirely red wines, but you will occasionally find a white example. The red is a blend of grenache rouge and grenache gris which gives finesse and elegance. This intense and yet often mysterious quality is coaxed out of the vines by the winds and mists of the Mediterranean.

Rivesaltes is a vast appellation that extends over both the Pyrénées-Orientales and the Aude regions. You can find examples in all three colours and the area offers a touch more creativity to its winemakers as the macabeu grape is allowed alongside grenache noir, gris and blanc. In the past, carignan was also widely used. Two main styles are found; pale amber in colour from a majority macebeu and grenache gris blend and the deeper brick style that has a higher proportion of grenache rouge.

Because of its sprawling nature, Rivesaltes has traditionally been the most difficult of the three appellations to market. Winemakers have tended to age the wines for many years in their cellars, often more by necessity than desire, particularly when markets are particularly tough. It's perhaps not always great for their businesses, but it has meant many families are able to pass on their treasures from one generation to the next. The large-size oak casks where the wines are stored are lightly porous and allow a gentle oxygen exchange between the wine and the surrounding atmosphere. This slow oxidation is an excellent technique for aging.

From an early age my father taught me how to taste these wines, particularly those from Mas Sauvy, known for its remarkable Rivesaltes made according to the solera system as in Jerez de la Frontera in Spain, where fortified sherry wines are slowly but surely blended together to ensure a consistent taste between each bottling. As I grew older, I never lost the habit of tasting and delighting in these wines whenever I was in the Roussillon.

In the early 1990s, I was told that there was a large amount of the 1974 vintage of Rivesaltes available in the cooperative cellars of Terrats. I headed over there, tasted, and decided to buy. From this decision, we began to produce our own Rivesaltes, starting with 200,000 bottles of this delectable 1974 vintage. Within two years, it was sold out. We had developed a premium category for these wines and at the same time brought them to the attention of a wider world.

Later, I visited Madame Villa, a charming and enthusiastic woman who allowed us to buy 4,000 bottles of her stunning 1959. She had carefully guarded this wine in her cellars for more than 40 years because her husband had told her it was an exceptional vintage. We in turn shared it with some of the world's best restaurants and it was such a success that within three years every bottle had gone. Not for long, because a change of importer in Denmark meant that I had to buy back some stock, and I was thrilled to discover 120 bottles of the 1959 in a cellar in Copenhagen. I could only thank Providence.

These wines stir deep emotions in me. They are a rare witness to generations past, an ancestral know-how and a touching humility; truly a moving combination. They can be drunk before, during or after a meal, but are perhaps best enjoyed in moments of quiet solitude, when you can be at one with the glass, quietly meditating on all that they represent.

I love, as the evening draws in after a summer's day, to find a quiet spot in the garden and pour a drop of Rivesaltes 1945. The first sip transports me, as the whispers of the wine entwine with my wandering thoughts. I can feel my spirits lifting, as I commune with the beauty of nature and give thanks for the beauty of the moment. This wine is a flag in the sands of time. For me 1945 represents the triumph of forces for good, liberty restored, the thrill of a new world, the potential for throwing off the bonds of fear and terror.

Marcel Rouillé, my friend and fellow Catalan, has spent 40 years of his life making some of the greatest wines of Roussillon, and developing a close relationship and understanding with its winemakers. His understanding of these wines is rivaled only by that of the other great oenologist of Roussillon, Jean Rière–who has just handed over the torch to my talented school friend Jean-Michel Barcelo. Before Marcel began to think about retiring, I asked him to help me with an important mission. Together, over 10 years, we patiently visited countless cellars to create a collection of vintage Rivesaltes. We followed recommendations, clues and chance conversations along voyages of discovery that were timeless and unusual. With the help and expertise of our own talented oenologist

Stéphane Quéralt–also originally from Roussillon–we uncovered a cellar that had been untouched for 25 years, ever since the owner had lost his keys.

The result of our searching was more than I could have ever hoped for. Today we have a collection of 19 vintages dating from 1977 back to 1875. Two centuries of history, legends, happiness and suffering are contained in these bottles.

We tasted all of these wines from the cask, and then bottled them ourselves with the greatest care. My intention is to sell only a small fraction over the rest of my career, and to leave the majority of the bottles to future generations, who will in turn continue the tradition and help to deliver a message that reveals the soul of our region.

32

A Thousand and One Details

From youth to experience

Cap Insula is the symbol of our deep roots in La Clape, originally known as *Insula lec*. It is also a place, a finger of land where our new cellars join the Mediterranean Sea. In the heart of 23 hectares of vines, Cap Insula creates a link between the winemaking heritage and the recent renewal of our region.

The intention with building these cellars is to make the best wines that we can, wines for the new century, while still respecting our ancestors and all they have taught us. We want to use modern winemaking, aging and bottling techniques in the service of capturing the originality of these lands and offering consumers across all continents the chance to open bottles in the best conditions, wherever they are.

It takes patience, maturity and a great deal of rigour to produce a great wine. But it also takes a shared vision across an entire team, and a sense of intuition that compels you to first search out and then reveal the soul of a specific *terroir*. It is a road that is full of obstacles, where the view is set according to the changing seasons.

It is essential to remain humble and open to nature, because she will tell you what she needs. If you impose your own desire or a pre-chosen set of techniques you will never hear what the land is saying. The vine is nothing without its roots–the magic happens underground, out of sight. The plant in this way becomes a symbol of the human body, where the roots are legs, carrying messages between the soil and the grapes, nourishing them and transmitting cosmic forces.

The trunk is the visible part, immutable, protected by bark that, just like skin, dries out and becomes replenished over the course of the years. The trunk almost always grows straight, but sometimes its form is torturous, knotted and gnarled. It is the backbone of a plant that can sometimes twist and turn, like a scoliosis. The influence and force of the wind will have an impact, and a vineyard can be read like the pages of a book, the direction of its trunk pointing to the dominant influence of the wind.

We have 13 different winds in the Narbonne region: the wind that blows from the south; the Spanish wind; the cold tramontane from the north; the Carcassès wind; the dry wind called Cers; the north wind; the Saint-Porais; the south-easterly Autan wind; the Greek wind; the Narbonnais; the sea breeze; the eastern wind and the wind that blows in from the causses. All have an influence on the growth of the vine and the character of the vintage.

Finally the branches, or *sarments*, that grow from the *souquets*–the Occitan word for vine stock–represent the arms, hands and fingers. Flowers appear at their tips in springtime, soon to transform into tiny buds and onwards into fruit. Slowly the grapes will take on their final shape, colour and size, through a slow process of development and ripening. The leaves, which capture the sun's energy through photosynthesis, are also nurtured by welcoming influences of rain and air. The grape will also be influenced by the aromas of neighbouring plants–cistus, olive trees, truffle trees, mulberry bushes, broom, thyme and rosemary.

Understanding the biosphere in which the vine grows means developing a respect for a natural way of farming. The presence of a wide variety of trees is therefore essential to the overall harmony of a wine estate. Wine growers must respect the balance of nature if it exists on their arrival, or re-create it if it has been lost. Doing so ensures the fertility of the earth and guarantees to the next generation that there will still be life in the soil. The winemaker is a benefactor of humanity, because through his presence, his work, the precision of his gestures, he protects the earth that nourishes us and promotes harmony in the world.

Pruning the vines carries a deep significance because it is through this task of cutting away the dead wood each winter that the vine plant is renewed and regenerated, creating the promise of a new season, where flowers will bloom in preparation for the harvest to come. We can only respect and wonder at this immutable process, the perfect circle of nature's wisdom.

An old vine, sometimes one hundred years old, will have kept generations of winemakers company. And it will continue to send out its message and its poetry over many decades through the bottles of wine that were made by its fruit. The best way to listen to these messages is through a vertical tasting of wines from a specific property, which allows us to drink with emotion, reading the story of its life in the glasses.

Wine is bottled time, even as time itself passes inexorably. It is the only drink from a perennial plant that has the virtue of coming from a specific area, sometimes even a specific plot of land, and yet offering up such an infinite variety of tastes. Through the communion with a great bottle of wine we get closer to an understanding of magic, of alchemy, of love. Wine lovers search out these moments where they can be transported for a few moments, or a few hours, to another universe, where they can share a moment of grace.

The winemaker must master all the myriad stages of winemaking, from the moment of harvest to the shipping of the final product, passing by vinification, aging, blending and bottling. We return here to the "thousand and one details" that were so dear to my father. My experience, shared with my winemaking friends and colleagues, tells me that repeatedly tasting the grapes in each plot is the best way to test not only their ripeness and quality potential but also their phenolic maturity–the state of evolution of their skin and pips. You need to study the colour of the pips and crunch them between your teeth. A ripe pip changes colour from green to brown; it offers little resistance as you bite down into it. It can either be a friend or enemy to the wine–if it is not ripe enough it can impart bitter flavours that are responsible for an astringent taste in the mouth, particularly in red wine that undergoes maceration of its juice with the skins and pips.

Once the grapes are safely brought into the cellar, vinification starts, during which the cellar master follows and influences rather than directs. There are no magicians in the cellars, only men who think well, and deeply, and are guided by their intuition.

After this comes the blending, the determining step in the composition of a wine. It is the single most important act in the entire chain, from pruning to bottling. It is the moment that the character of a wine is revealed. It must harness the essence of both the vintage and the *terroir*.

The blending of different plots is the work of a master, requiring solid experience and a good understanding of a vineyard and a region if he is to avoid standardised wines, with neither emotion nor soul, even if technically well made.

Taking into account the hierarchy in the pyramid of the senses, the consumer can choose their wine by following the steps of pleasure, taste, emotion and message, and through this enter the closed world of the erudite, those who are not satisfied with simple tastes but who search for complexity, the fruit of wisdom, inspiration and the sign of a winemaker's skill.

I recently had the great privilege to meet the extraordinary Japanese writer Katsumi Tanaka, a great expert on biodynamics and lover of French wine. He has spent part of his life working in the kitchens of a New York restaurant and is always keen to pierce through the mysteries of wine to uncover its true potential, verticality and vibrations, in search of the musicality of wine, delivered by its symphony of colours, aromas and tastes.

Katsumi has notably succeeded in understanding the importance of the blending in the balance that it brings to wine. When tasting, he searches for a wine's melody, resonance and inner harmony. He defines the structure of a wine like that of a temple, with a foundation, structure, body and roof.

Wines from different vats will enter into one of these categories. The implication of the temple is that there is also a divine proportion between one and another. It is possible to draw a comparison with the great painters of the Renaissance who added gold leaf to their canvases. Leonardo da Vinci was one of the most influential proponents of this careful, painstaking technique that conveyed purity and a sign of religious faith. The search for perfection and excellence–in the architecture of temples, in great art and in the blending of wine–is often based on the principles of mathematics.

The blending session often confirms and explains what we already instinctively know. The ultimate objective is for the wine to be multi-dimensional, mouth-filling and a link between the senses, the heart and the neo-cortex. This is achieved by balance, uniting aromas, structure, texture and minerality. Once the perfect proportions have been uncovered, aging allows the tannins in red wine to soften, and it lets the white wines gain in refinement.

The choice of barrels is key. Over the years, Jean-Claude Berrouet shared his experience and his knowledge with me over the choice of oak, the level of toasting of the staves, the width of the grain, the length of time the barrel should be left to dry and season after the tree is felled and the origin of the wood. The barrels themselves have to be prepared before being filled with wine. It is a precise ceremony that involves rinsing the barrels with clear water to eliminate any excess of tannins. After a few days, the water has taken on some of the colour of the oak, oscillating between green and brown, and once finished, the barrels are ready to receive the wine. For white wines, barrel aging in our estates lasts between 6 and 8 months, and for the reds at least 12 months. The tannins in the wine will gently form an exchange of characteristics with those of the wood, and will lengthen, refine and gain in complexity, elegance and finesse. Wood has replaced the ancient earthenware pots used in antiquity to transport wine, because its porosity favours what is known as controlled oxidation–a gentle exchange between wine, oak and air. After aging, each barrel is tasted and assessed to ensure there have been no issues such as bacterial spoilages.

Once everything is assured, the final step is to create the master blend in large vats, transposing the work in the laboratory to the final wine, and to prepare for bottling. The process is the same for all our wines, whether for daily drinking wines or exceptional rare bottles. The charm of this industry is that every wine demands careful analysis and an individual treatment. There is no such thing as a cookie-cutter approach. Each wine is by its very nature one-of-a-kind and deserves to be treated as such.

In recognition of this philosophy, our new wine cellar was conceived around the pursuit of excellence. We chose an architect who shared our values and who listened to our needs. Jean-Frédéric Luscher was selected after a bidding process. His designs won through their suggestion of a building in the form of an H–standing for harmony, hedonism and hospitality. The configuration of the building, which was built according to strict environmental norms, ensures an excellent flow of energy and respects the building theories behind ancient temples, ensuring the balance between cosmic and earthly forces and allowing the wines to receive the necessary messages before bottling. The roof of the winery is made of natural wood, the foundations and floor of brushed concrete and brick–all materials that favour interactions.

Each temple, church or cathedral is built to soothe men and women and bring them closer to God, and so to the universe. Similarly there is a sacred dimension, a spiritual joy in this building. The equipment in the cellar is perfectly adapted to the tasks at hand, ensuring bottling is a smooth and peaceful process.

After bottling, and a few weeks rest, the wines are ready to be sent to our clients around the world to begin their journey as chroniclers of the character of our lands.

33

Extending a Hand to the Future

Sine vino vana hospitalitas. There is no hospitality without wine. This is the motto that embodies the values of our group, of our teams and of our *art de vivre*.

I write this as I approach my fiftieth birthday, the midway point of life. I have fulfilled my need to look inwards and to share with you the path of discovery that has led me here. The years from being a child in Corbières to being a responsible adult have passed all too quickly. It seemed essential for me to take stock, to make sense of the life that was thrust on me following the sudden death of my father on October 28, 1987. Because beyond the love, admiration and respect that I have always had for my parents, and the deep connection to my father Georges, it seemed essential, vital even, to examine the path that I have taken. I wanted to be certain that I would have followed it even if my father had been still with us. Without any doubt, my life would have been different. It is sometimes difficult to find your place next to your father, particularly when he is a mentor and boss as mine was. But I am certain that he would have given me the space and independence to find my own way and to grow into myself at his side, benefitting from his experience. Life decided otherwise.

Accepting my destiny, I took over the reins of the family estate with determination, passion and ambition while still leaving enough energy to pursue my dreams of rugby. For the first few years, my father was there to guide and inspire me. Even after his loss, I missed him, but at some level he was, and is, never truly absent. The continued feeling of his presence has led me to think about life and death, and what waits for us beyond. It has given me great strength. I am convinced at the most profound level that there are no accidents but that there is a meaning, sometimes hidden, in everything.

We need to find the right key to unlock the door to our own path and to living a full life. To do so takes confidence and a willingness to commit. As Nelson Mandela wrote, "Our deepest fear is not that we are inadequate. Our deepest fear is that we are powerful beyond measure. It is our light, not our darkness that most frightens us. We ask ourselves, *Who am I to be brilliant, gorgeous, talented, fabulous?* Actually, who are you not to be? You are a child of God. We were born to make manifest the glory of God that is within us. It is not just in some of us; it is in everyone. And as we let our own light shine, we unconsciously give other people permission to do the same".

There is something mysterious about this journey I have taken, as if it has been guided by a higher wisdom, and at times it has seemed almost mystical. Rugby built me, wine gave me faith. Synchronicity and providence sent me the right people and opportunities along the way to open my eyes and to allow me to keep growing and evolving.

I stopped playing professional rugby in 1994, just before my thirtieth birthday, and turned to focus all my energies on the wine of my region. The first years of my wine career involved endless sleepless nights and plenty of soul-searching and self-doubt. Adrenaline, enthusiasm and the sheer excitement of attacking something new got me through. After five years, I began to feel more in control, finding my inner resources and my centre. I always had the desire to do well, but started to develop deeper skills and understanding.

Viticulture and oenology demand an unwavering commitment and focus that can develop into a form of clairvoyance. My father's words are always with me. "Wine is the result of a thousand-and-one details". Understanding teamwork, learning to delegate and building a strong sense of trust is also essential. Along the way I have learnt who I am and what my purpose is. This knowledge has not only brought me peace, but also given me the desire to create in my turn, and to share the *terroir* and culture of our region in France and abroad. Winemaking gives you a continual sense of humility; linked as it is to the capriciousness of the climate, the will of nature and the mysterious alchemy needed to make great wines.

"If you want a straight furrow, hitch your wagon to a star", wrote Antoine de Saint-Exupéry. This metaphor perfectly sums up my vision of winemaking. I hope that I may continually oscillate between very good, excellent and exceptional wines. Excellence is my guide, the path that I try to follow. It is sometimes demanding not only for me, but also for my colleagues. But that is simply the price you pay to produce wine year after year, respecting the vintage character, while guaranteeing quality, a sense of place and a transmission of *savoir-faire*. This last part, *savoir-faire* or know-how, is essential, but so is its alter ego, *faire-savoir,* or sharing knowledge. It is the only way to engage in sincere experiences with clients and consumers.

I hope to continue to live fully engaged in the creation of wines that stand witness to the South of France, and to share them, and our life here, with those who love them. I hope to continue to educate, to pass on the history, culture and atmosphere of the Mediterranean civilisation.

All who want to share this human adventure are welcome. We are lucky enough to be witnessing the birth of a new paradigm, and I hope that together we will continue to celebrate the joy that these wines can bring, and the joy of the South of France.

Postface

Finding happiness through taking action

I often say that happiness lies in taking positive action and meeting Gérard proved to me once again how true this is. He has the energy and contagious enthusiasm of someone who is committed to making a difference in this world. He brilliantly combines being a gifted evangelist, spreading the gospel of biodynamics across his estates, with being a successful businessman who has turned his dreams into reality. And all of this wrapped up in such charisma that it is impossible to meet him without wanting to try his wines.

Like all winemakers, he creates something more powerful than simply a drink containing alcohol : he brings pleasure and happiness. The true importance of this was brutally brought home to me ten years ago in New Orleans when the helicopter that I was travelling in crashed. I was certain that I was going to die and cried with joy when I realised that I had been spared. The first things I asked for were a phone to call my wife... and a glass of wine. Because in that Anglo-Saxon world, a stranger surrounded by medical professionals in an unknown hospital, wine made me think of my friends and my country. I wanted to feel close to things that were important to me and that would give me comfort – and wine embodies this.

Friendship, sharing, the joy of being with others and opening up to them, all this is part of the universe of wine – just as it is part of the motivation behind sustainable development. Gérard feels as I do ; that ecology is above all humanism ; a love song because to protect the planet we first of all need to love it. More than words, this shared belief is something that our friendship has been built upon.

Today Gérard has chosen to support my foundation GoodPlanet – so called because it tries to bring out the good that exists on this Earth. And I thank him warmly.

Each copy sold of this book will help finance projects to raise awareness of ecology and promote a way of life that is respectful of the Earth and its inhabitants. I hope that knowledge will bring you – beyond the pleasure of reading – the satisfaction of contributing towards making our world a better place.

Yann Arthus-Bertrand,
President of the GoodPlanet Foundation

Selective bibliography

Klein, Étienne, *Petit voyage dans le monde des quanta,* éditions Flammarion
Ortoli, Sven and Pharabod, Jean-Pierre, *Le Cantique des quantiques* éditions de la Découverte
Steiner, Rudolf, *Agriculture Course: The Birth of the Biodynamic Method*, Rudolph Steiner Press
W. Hawking, Stephen, *A Brief History of Time: From the Big Bang to Black Holes*, Bantal Dell Publishing Group
Zeland, Vadim, *Reality Transurfing, The Space of Variations*, O Books

Photos credits

Page 188 : Pied de Vigne ©William Moulin
Numbers 1-21, 31, 32, 37-39 : ©Gérard Bertrand Archives
Numbers 22-30, 33 : ©Gilles Deschamps
Numbers 34-36, 40-42 : ©Soufiane Zaidi
Number 43 : ©Fabrice Leseigneur
Pages XXII-XXIV : ©Professeur Georges Vieilledent

I - Getting Started

II - The Estates

III - The Terroirs

IV - Back to the Future

Gérard Bertrand

Wine, Moon and Stars

1

2

3

1. Gérard's grandmother, Paule
2. Georges and Geneviève, his parents, on their wedding day
3. With his sister, Guylaine

4

5

6

4. Ingrid, Gérard, Emma and Mathias
5. Georges in a tasting session
6. George and Gérard on holidays
7. Emma Bertrand tastes the grapes during the harvest
8. Mathias Bertrand tastes the grapes during the harvest

7

8

9

10

11

9. Gérard's first match for Saint-André
10. The team that Gérard's father coached, champions of the France Honneur competition
11. Narbonne's team the day they won the Challenge Yves de Manoir
12. France VII team in Hong-Kong

12

13

13. The Knights of the *Art de Vivre*
14. Gérard and his friend Jean-Luc Piquemal
15. Yann Arthus-Bertrand, Jean-Pierre Rives and Gérard at the *Art de Vivre* Festival

16

17

16. Jacques Michaud
17. Gérard's friends: Yuri Buenaventura, Claude Spanghero, Richard Astre and Didier Codorniou
18. The Jazz Festival
19. The Breitling Patrol in a demonstration, at the Château L'Hospitalet

18

19

20

21

20. Château de Quéribus
21. Château de Peyrepertuse
22. Domaine Cigalus
23. Château Laville-Bertrou
24. Château L'Hospitalet
25. Domaine de l'Aigle

22

23

24

25

26

27

28

26. Château Aigues-Vives ageing cellar
27. Château La Sauvageonne
28. Château La Soujeole
29. L'Hospitalitas
30. La Forge
31. Château Les Karantes

29

30

31

32

32. Le Viala
33. Clos d'Ora vineyard
34. Vineyard Team
35. Enlarged Managing Team
36. United States Team

33

34

35

36

37

38

37. Gérard with Jean-Claude Berrouet, Gyslain Coux and Jean-Baptise Terlay in a testing session
38. Marc Dubernet and Gérard in the cellar
39. Gérard and his friend Tanaka
40. Cap Insula, exterior view
41. Cap Insula, interior view
42. Clos d'Ora, the cellar

40

41

42

43. Clos d'Ora 2012, first vintage

Gérard Bertrand

Quantum wine

In order to better understand my intuition regarding wine's ability to transmit messages, I met with a team of French researchers whose work has long appealed to me. For the first time I was able to concretely see the different informational fields in wine.

I am sharing a few of the resulting images with you. We cannot fully do them justice here and more research is needed, yet they reveal the force and beauty which all natural beings emit.

The technique is used by researchers at a company called Electrophotonique Ingenierie, and is headed up by Georges Vieilledent. It uses macroscopic images showing the electromagnetic waves given out by different beings and objects. It is an entirely new technique to measure the previously invisible fields around us all, revealing the energy or vitality of a body submerged in an electromagnetic field by showing the vibrations given out by specific samples of – in this case – wine.

I have witnessed the results and will allow Vieilledent to explain exactly how it works.

'A single drop of wine is drawn up into a pipette and placed in suspension on a transparent electrode. The lights are switched off in the laboratory and an electromagnetic field is generated, which in turn creates what is known as a corona effect, or a discharge of energy that is visible and glows like a halo around the drop of wine. The technique is well known to scientists, and has been used by several industries except that, in this case, the quality of the pictures produced reveals details of the bioluminescence in ways that have never been discovered before. The corona effect is then captured under UV light by a special scientific camera with an extremely high-resolution lens.

The result of this picture process is remarkable. In just a few seconds, the high-definition lens allows you to see your wine in an entirely new way, through a multitude of information, colours and shapes that are beautiful and illuminating. But the energetic signature that the image reveals is also perfectly quantifiable, even if complex, and reveals the system's entropy through highlighting its smallest, most subtle properties.

The potential of this technique is threefold:

— Through the use of macroscopic imagery, we are able to observe the quantum energy of an object. This means witnessing complex electromagnetic and electrostatic fields that are essentially packets of energy exchanged as the object emits or absorbs light according to the frequency of its vibrations. This is quantum energy.

— The electric field produced by the process is stablised, which means that it is possible to discover ever more precise indications about the physical and chemical stability of the sample under observation. Further studies are needed here but we are looking at unveiling the specific vibratory field of an object – information that can eventually reveal to us the deepest secrets of existence.

— Like sound waves, light can also transmit specific information – an exchange takes place between two beings capable of understanding the message. Television is the most obvious example of this, where sound and image are used to diffuse all types of messages to a wide audience. At its heart, it is a simple question of waves.

With the corona effect, the spatial and geometric information given through the photonic flux reveals similarly concrete messages. The key is to understand where this message is coming from and what it is telling us.

Without becoming too technical, there are three key elements within this photonic image that help to explain my theory of quantum wine.

The energetic signature of the Corona Effect

Observe the density, regularity and extension of the corona of Clos d'Ora 2012 compared to the second wine.

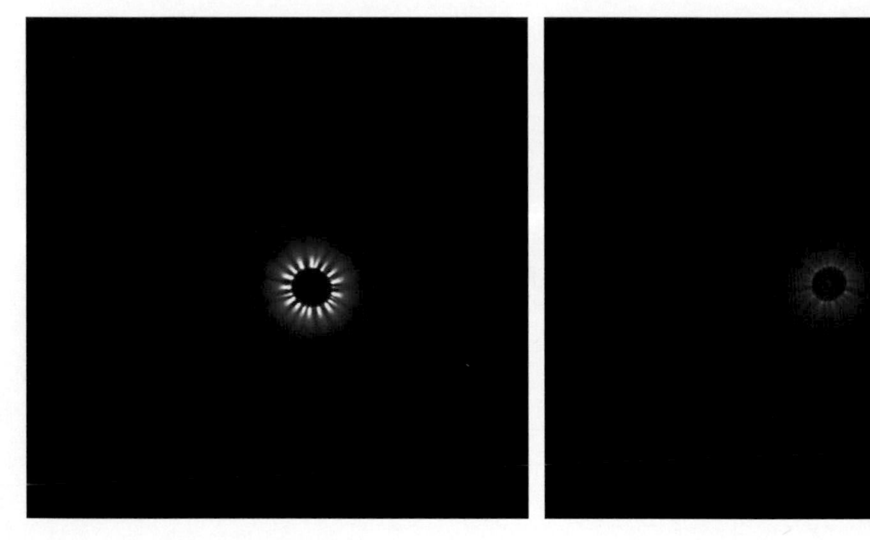

Clos d'Ora 2012 — Conventional wine

The stability of the photonic flux

Observe the difference between the Clos d'Ora 2012 produced under biodynamic farming conditions and that more 'misty' flux of the second wine, produced with conventional agriculture.

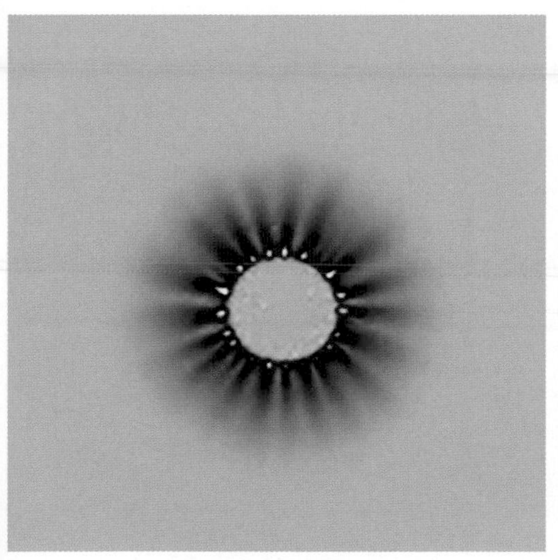

Clos d'Ora 2012

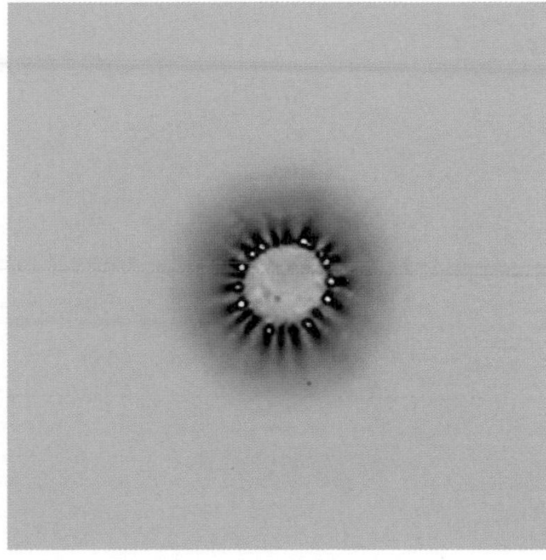

Conventional wine

The spatial layout

Observe the perfect uniformity of the photonic flux in the Clos d'Ora 2013.

Clos d'Ora 2013, sample 1
(barrel aged brut)

Clos d'Ora 2013, sample 2
(barrel aged brut)